G000277404

NATIONAL MARITIME MUSEUM

Voyaging With The Wind

AN INTRODUCTION TO SAILING LARGE SQUARE-RIGGED SHIPS

ALAN VILLIERS

LONDON : HER MAJESTY'S STATIONERY OFFICE

First published 1975

ISBN 0 11 880758 7

Contents

Preface

THE business of handling large square-rigged ships is not to be learned by reading but by doing. Now that the doing is all but impossible, this brief work is offered more as an introduction to a very large subject, a departed way of seafaring life, than any sort of comprehensive text-book. A list of some of these (for what they may now be worth) is given in an appendix. They were helpful to those who already knew the subject from their own practical experience. They were intended to help these in their examinations for advancement in a profession they had mastered the only real way there was.

All the photographs in this book, except that of the *Preussen*, were taken by myself.

ALAN VILLIERS

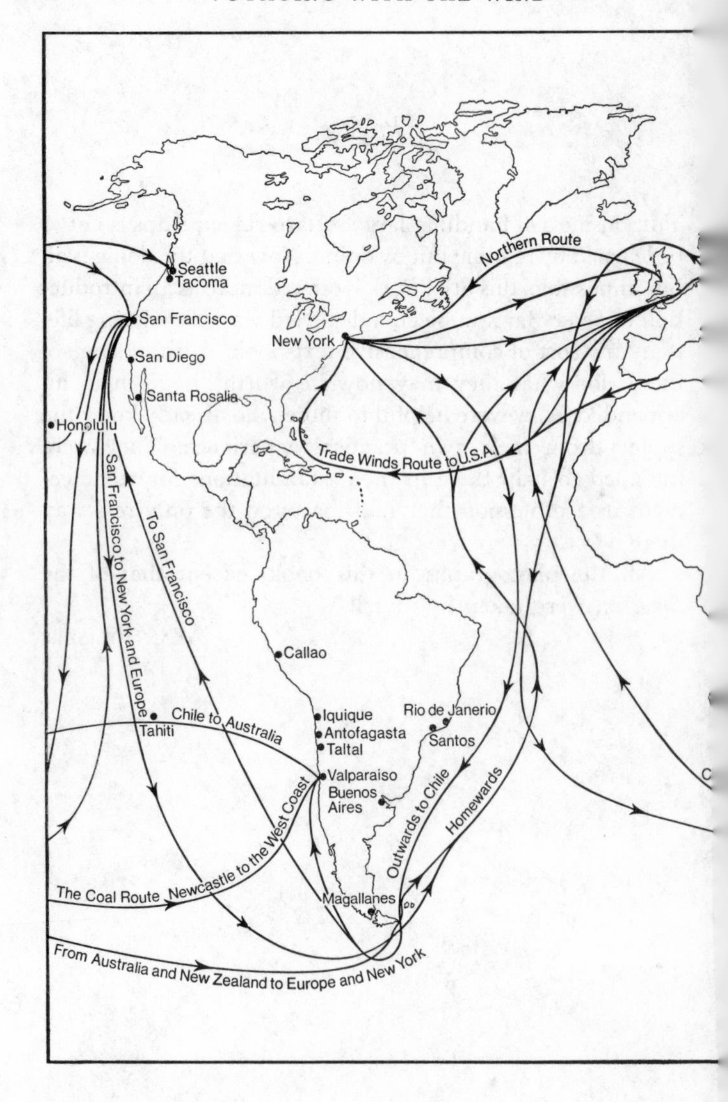

Sailing-ship routes of the world, and the great sea ports.

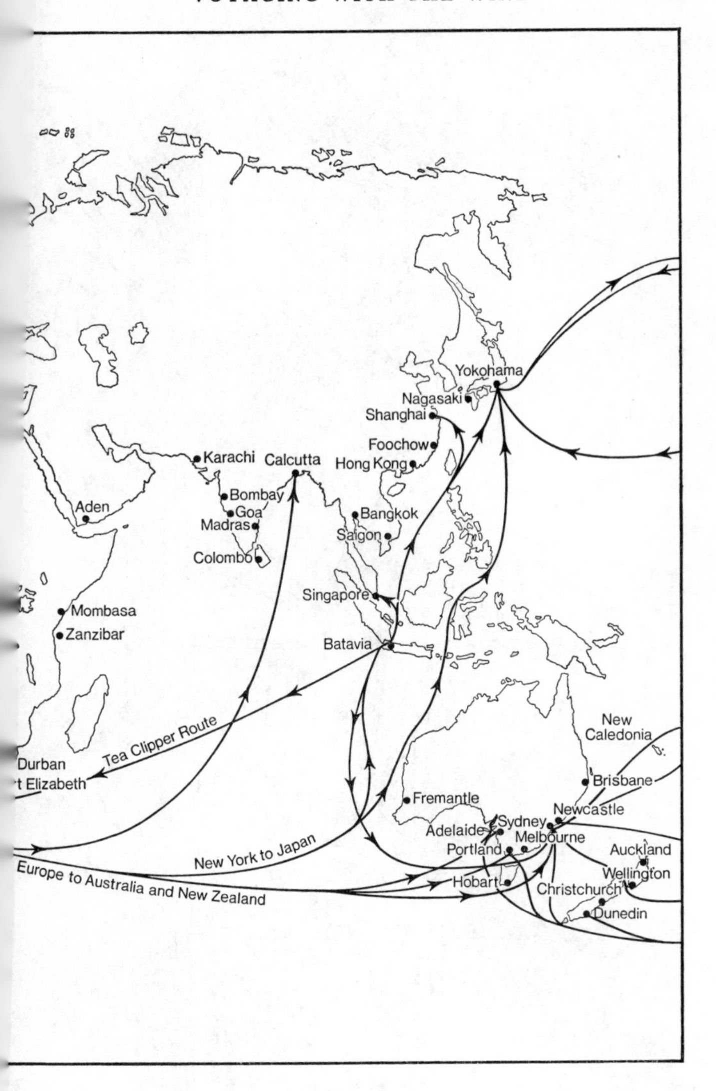
Yokohama
Nagasaki
Shanghai
Foochow
Hong Kong
Karachi
Calcutta
Aden
Bombay
Goa
Madras
Bangkok
Saigon
Colombo
Singapore
Mombasa
Zanzibar
Batavia
Tea Clipper Route
Durban
t Elizabeth
New Caledonia
Brisbane
Fremantle
Newcastle
Sydney
Adelaide
Melbourne
Portland
Auckland
Wellington
Hobart
Christchurch
Dunedin
New York to Japan
Europe to Australia and New Zealand

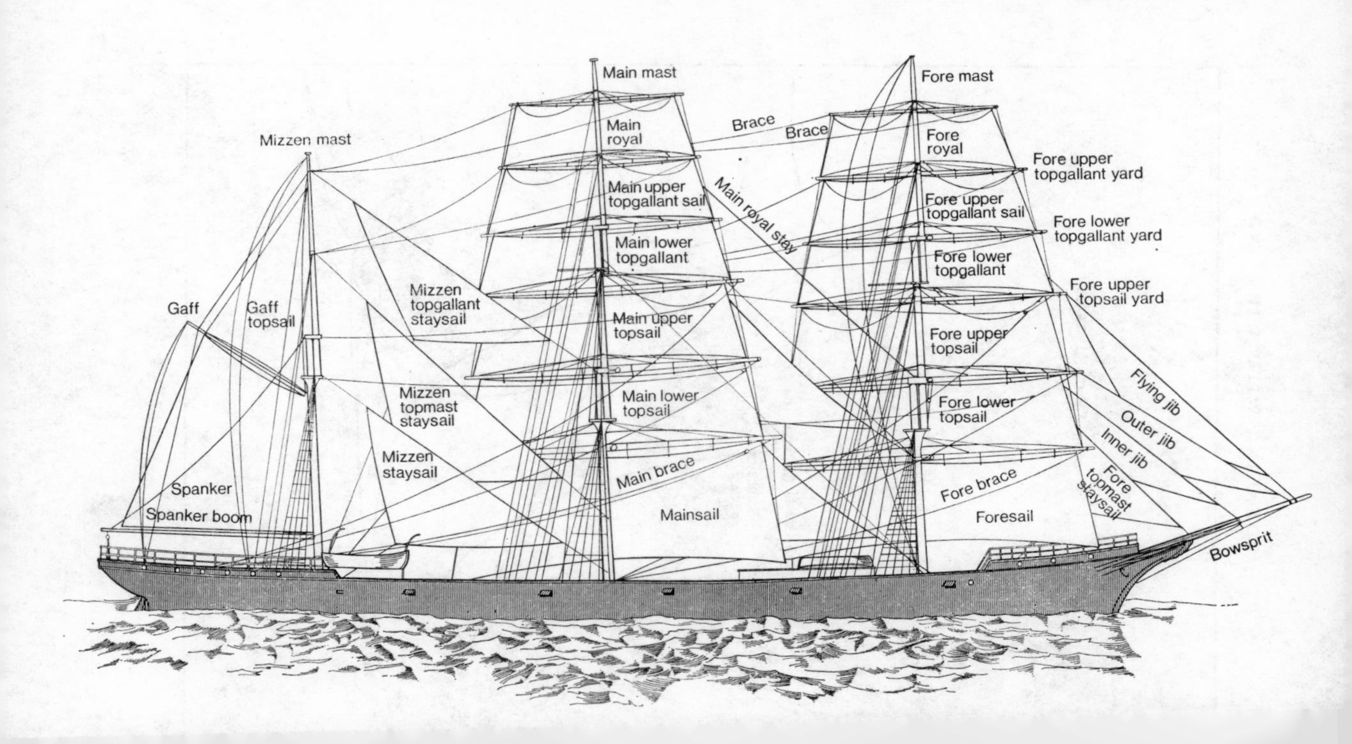

Main mast
Fore mast
Mizzen mast
Main royal
Brace
Brace
Fore royal
Fore upper topgallant yard
Main upper topgallant sail
Main royal stay
Fore upper topgallant sail
Fore lower topgallant yard
Main lower topgallant
Fore lower topgallant
Fore upper topsail yard
Mizzen topgallant staysail
Gaff
Gaff topsail
Main upper topsail
Fore upper topsail
Flying jib
Mizzen topmast staysail
Main lower topsail
Fore lower topsail
Outer jib
Inner jib
Mizzen staysail
Main brace
Fore brace
Fore topmast staysail
Spanker
Spanker boom
Mainsail
Foresail
Bowsprit

I

The Square-Rigged Ship & Her Seamen – The Background

THERE were two fundamental and separate skills which a deep-sea square-rigged ship master had to acquire – first, to understand and look after the ship and all her gear, sails, tackle and rigging (to say nothing of the care of her compasses and charts, the health and morale of her crew, provisioning and all that) and secondly, to sail her as an expert ship-handler and voyage-maker, intelligently, with at least a good working knowledge of the behaviour of the principal ocean winds and currents, the best ways to get across the oceans and round the world using only the wind in the sails. Both these skills took time to master – three or four years for the first, half-a-lifetime for the second. No one could just step aboard a big barque or full-rigged ship and handle and sail her, for she was a complicated structure and could be awkward and vulnerable. But as long as the ships themselves lasted as real engine-less working ships (which was into the 1950's) the long-fostered know-how and traditions of their handling and passage-making lasted too, with unbroken continuity. They were not maintained by full-powered 'school' or training ships, no matter what rigging these also had. Many of these did, and still do, a useful job in their own right: none was conceived for carrying-on working square-rigger knowledge, but to be – usually – part of some academic training ashore where it was of necessity based; or, as with the Scandinavians, for the indoctrination of young merchant seamen to their demanding profession. The nearest approaches to real square-rigger sailing today are to be found in Denmark and Norway, for these countries train boys in their four full-rigged ships the whole spring, summer, and autumn – time enough to learn something properly.

At first glance either at a model or one of the ships themselves, the big square-rigged ship looked a highly complicated piece of work. The maze of rigging growing in profusion from the long sweep of graceful decks, the high masts with their enormous yards, the fragile tracery of the lighter running rigging high aloft – how could man ever handle such creations, make profitable voyages in them of reasonably predictable length, and go on doing such things year after year? With a handful of youth for crew, watchkeeping officers in their late 'teens or early twenties, the bare minimum of experienced crew and, like as not, the bare minimum of everything else, too? How did they get on when they had to beat their way into foul winds? How could they claw off a lee shore, fight their way to wind'ard past the Horn, and survive in the midwinter gales of that most vicious of all oceans, the North Atlantic? How, indeed, did they dare to go to sea at all?

Big square-rigged ships were, in fact, most interesting, ingenious, and when properly handled, highly effective pieces of engineering. As long as they lasted, they were handled by men who grew up in them, starting young – very young, by today's standards – and lived in them on voyages which often lasted years. The road to command was hard and highly selective. From the first moment of coming aboard until the last hour in command, the *whole* of the ship and her workings were in the full sight of everyone – and very often at sea, nothing else was. A boy living day after day, week after week, year after year in a ship like that soon knew her.

Square-rigged ships varied in rig, number of masts, number of sails on the masts, but essentially they were all rigged in the same manner. The apparent complication of both standing and running rigging was really orderly and quite straightforward to those who lived with it. All sails had much the same gear, led much the same way. A sailor from Drake's *Golden Hind* would soon understand the lead of the gear in the *Victory* and be a useful hand aboard on his first sea watch: a sailor from the *Victory*, though perhaps appalled at first by the size of everything and the complication of double topsails and topgallants, would rapidly know his way round such a ship as the four-masted barque *Herzogin Cecilie*. Square-rigged ships followed one another down the ways in orderly evolution from the beginning to the end of their days. It was a slow evolution. Men could keep up with it.

The same thing worked the other way. When my crew and I had to sail the replica *Mayflower* from Plymouth, Devon, across the North Atlantic in 1957, it took less than a watch for the Cape Horner men aboard – the three watchkeeping officers, and a handful of the mariners – to understand the 'drill' for the effective handling of her 16th century spritsail, the deep topsails set from slight yards, the main course with its bonnet and its lack of reef-points, the awkward lateen sail on the mizzen-mast. Once we had worked out the best ways to handle all this and get the ship along efficiently, the rest of the crew quickly caught on. We found that spritsail, set far ahead on the long bowsprit, to be a sail of such effectiveness in manoeuvre that I wondered why it had ever been given up for the less efficient jibs, though the unstayed bowsprit could wave like a wand in strong winds. The spritsail offset the windage of the high poop, and that poop acted as a storm trysail when necessary, to heave the ship to under no sail at all.

Of course, like this she just drifted, but not fast. She lay-to very easy in the sea as a good ship should when she can't go. Her hull and her sails were simple but efficient, when understood. Her masts worked a lot with their cordage rigging, and this at first alarmed those used to the rigid modern Cape Horners with their all-steel masts and yards and iron-wire rigging. We soon perceived that their capacity for 'give' made the *Mayflower's* masts able to accept the stresses and shocks of working in the sea. If they had been rigid, they might have gone over the side.

So long as ocean-going square-riggers lasted, the traditions of accepting and handling them lasted, too. They were served by men who understood them. Their slow evolution matched the slow growth in knowledge of another kind – the behaviour of the ocean winds. The wind might blow 'where it listeth' but ocean winds have roughly defined zones, patterns of behaviour, and movements. Man had to have a good idea of these before he could wander off in square-rigged ships across the face of the earth. I often think that Columbus' great achievement was not in stumbling more or less fortuitously upon the fringing tropic islands of the great American continents, but in blazing the sailing way across the North Atlantic. His Trade Winds run, from the Canaries to the West Indies, was the classic way to make westing in that ocean, and his passage back to Europe in the Gulf Stream drift beyond the Trades – north of them – was a fair semblance of the best way to sail eastwards there, too. It is a reasonable seamanlike assumption that Columbus would never have tried such a voyage had he not had prior knowledge of the winds and currents which made it possible. We write a lot about him, but we do not know what knowledge was available to him. We hear of him busily in search of it in Lisbon and elsewhere, long before the *Santa Maria* voyage.

Columbus' ship was a straightforward, uncomplicated little thing with few sails. So was the *Mayflower II*. By the 19th century the big square-rigger was much more complicated, but she never had evolved in a hurry, never so fast that all concerned could not keep up with her even in the galloping half-century from 1850 to 1900, which spanned the great development from, say, a Swansea copper-ore man of 1850, built of wood, carrying perhaps 400 tons, to the giant steel five-masted barque *Potosi* of the 1890's, carrying 6,000 tons, sailed by great masters from Robert Hilgendorf to Robert Miethe,* fighting her way to the westwards past the Horn, summer and winter, in a matter of days. The crew from the Swansea barque would have been very welcome,

* This grand old sea captain died in 1975, aged 97. He had been living not far from Valparaiso, at Quilpue in Chile.

and immediately competent aboard the *Potosi*. Wood to steel, rope to wire rigging, nine knots maximum to 16, 100-120-day passages cut to 70 between N. Europe and N. Chile, the ships were close relations, worked in fundamentally the same way just as in the tea clippers and Western Ocean packets too. 'Smart Alecs' or committees could not come along and change things round, because what had been slowly evolved was the best way of doing things – and the 'Smart Alecs' were not there.

These ships had no deck-lighting: their people had to know their ship's gear by feel and long-fostered knowledge. To make this practical, patterns of uniformity were developed especially with the sails and the running rigging necessary for their handling. For example, all sails were 'roped', i.e. sewn at their edges to strong hemp. This hemp was always sewn to the *after* sides of square sails, the *port* side of fore-and-afters. This helped when handling new sails out of the sail locker by night, to bend replacements, for the seamen always knew which way round the canvas must go. It was a big job to bend a new course or topsail and it had to be the right way round. By night seamen worked in the dark, for they had to preserve their night vision.

For the same common-sense reasons, the pattern of belaying-pins fore and aft was established and maintained, and the sail-handling gear that led to the deck (most did) led to the pins in an orderly and constant manner – not in precisely the same way in all ships, large and small, for some had more buntlines than others; some grouped course gear to pin-patterns each side round the bole of the mast, the others to the main pin-rails.* Winches or no winches, the style once

* With the later-day introduction of the Jarvis (Scots) hand-operated brace-winch on which brace-wires were led to three tapering drums on a small steel frame secured to the deck abaft the main, mizzen and jigger pinrails, and the German halliard winches which hoisted the heavier yards by stout single wire, there were some differences, because there was less gear to be used. Winch-handling was by handle. The winches were used in a minority of large ships only.

set up was rigidly maintained, and the general arrangement was much the same. Nothing was haphazard, and nothing was marked, either. What use were marks in the dark? What use was an ass who never learned his ship's gear? The sail-handling gear was always *grouped* in the same order – clewlines, buntlines, leechlines – so that their placings once learned in a ship the knowledge was readily retained. Clewlines hauled up the clews (corners) to the yardarms (or the quarter in older ships); buntlines hauled up the 'bunt', the great body of the sail, to the yard (the quarters in old-style ships). Hauled up in this manner, the square sail was said to be 'clewed up'. The idea was to make it manageable to the men strung out on footropes below the yard, in order that they might make a snug stow of the canvas and secure it with lighter lines called gaskets passed round a 'skin' of the sail – snugged up and smooth, so that strong wind would not find protruding folds to tear at. The men tackled the weather side of the sail first because it was more difficult: in older ships, they first fought the bunt, for in these the bunt was hauled up to the middle of the yard.

When the shout was 'All Hands!' and the midnight squall shrieked while the canvas thundered and the ship listed over, it was too late to grope for the proper belaying-pins. Same thing with all the gear – braces (the yard-swingers), halliards (the yard-hoisters), downhauls, sheets, tacks, the lot. There was defined and maintained order everywhere because it had 'grown up' that way in a man's world.

Nobody shone electric torches to spoil others' night vision. None had such torches. The first thing new hands did on joining was to learn the ropes – literally. In the same way, there was standardisation in the orders, which were both explicit and explanatory in minimum words. When men leapt into the rolling rigging to fight their way aloft and fist a wildly-flapping thundering sail, all knew exactly what they were at and how to go about it, under God. Which is not to say that such difficult and dangerous work was normally accomplished without a mighty tussle. It was not: but the tussle would have been much worse, if not often impossible, without this long-evolved system of tidiness – a place for everything and everything in its place: a name, a pin, a definite lead for everything. So it had to be, and so it was. The acquisition of all this knowledge had to be rapid and perfect. 'Knowing the ropes' was no figure of speech.

So also with the actual sail-handling and manoeuvring the yards, the sails, and the ship. As the wind altered in direction or force or both, it was necessary to trim the sails the better to use their power and get maximum forward way at all times without an undue strain on anything. As the wind headed (its direction drawing from further for'ard), the yards had to be hauled ('braced' was the word) more towards the ship's fore-and-aft line, to point up sharper. As the wind became more favourable, the yards had to be squared in, and the principal tacks and sheets trimmed. The wind had to be kept blowing into the sails from behind them, at the most efficient angle that the mate of the watch – he usually did the lesser bracing, which was an ever recurring job in any well-sailed ship – could judge. He was a good judge, or he wasn't a mate. There were explicit orders and procedures for all these manoeuvres. As the strength of the wind increased, sail area had to be reduced (for obviously an excess of wind-force abaft sails greater than was necessary to get best performance from them at the angle set, was merely a strain on the whole structure and no help to the ship at all): as it decreased, more sail could be set.

Like all else in the square-rigged ship, no manoeuvre was so unimportant that it could be set about wrongly: there was a right way to do everything. With fairing wind (its direction hauling-aft) the after-most yards were squared in first and most. With the wind heading, the for'ardest yards were trimmed first, and allowed to go nearest to the fore-and-aft line (always circumscribed by the angle of the essential standing rigging which limited their capacity to swing).

Everyone aboard knew these things, cook and steward included. There were standard orders for everything – 'Lee fore brace' for the heading wind, 'weather main brace' (or crojack in four-masted barques and full-rigged ships) for the wind shifting aft. Always the standard orders, well understood: always the thoroughly-comprehended manoeuvre, day or night – this was the way of it. Who could not or would not learn such elementary matters was of no use in a square-rigged ship and could, indeed, be a menace to his ship and shipmates, a one-passage lubber who soon went ashore and stayed there. You just had to have a good memory, be observant, and be nobody's fool.

There were regular terms of apprenticeship (called usually just 'time') to be served before advancement – first a year as deckboy, on deck, not flunkeying aft or loblollying in the galley, before advancement to ordinary seaman: two years more of that (also on deck, which included the whole of the rigging) before being considered fit to 'hand, reef, and steer' and to qualify as A.B.: maybe six to eight before becoming bos'n's mate for a big ship. Tradesmen such as carpenter, blacksmith (if carried: often the carpenter doubled in this capacity) and sailmaker had to serve at least seven years ashore in their trades before being allowed to stitch a seam or heat a caulking iron afloat.

As for officers – the all-important afterguard – advancement to third or perhaps second mate might be sought after four years before the mast or as an apprentice, on gaining the necessary certificate of competency by preparation while afloat, followed by cramming, and examination ashore. All sorts of subjects came into this, some of which did not bother a man much once he had passed in them, such as word-perfection in the international Rule of the Road, or an expert standard in signalling by morse and the international code of flags. The flags of the code were simple enough to memorise but a large book had to be consulted to look up the meaning of any hoist except a single flag. Each letter of the alphabet had its own meaning when hoisted alone. These could be memorised, and the four-flag hoist for the ship's identity. There was comparatively little signalling in big sailing merchantmen anyway, for they sailed alone – no fleets, no fleet manoeuvres. They had voyages to make and cargoes to deliver in as good order as possible. That was that, usually.

Recruitment to the afterguard was not normally from public school boys and never from universities. There was in Britain a system of apprenticeship under which boys of 14 and upwards to 16/17 could be bound to an owner, to work for him for four years in his ships for nothing (sometimes a pittance in the fourth year). The usual premium charged was £40 for each lad, which was a lot of money in 1895, or 1915. For this sum paid by their parents, four, six or eight hardy lads slept in a steel 'house' in the wettest part of the ship, where they had rough bunks, their own sea chests to sit on and their strict allowance of food like the foremast hands. Some ships were worse than others, but often the boys had not enough to eat at sea or in port. Instruction was minimal, if there was any. Far too many lads suffered serious injury or were lost, individually or the lot together, with their ship. The life was dangerous, although so readily acceptable – possibly because those big Cape Horn ships looked what they were, challenging and adventurous. Adventurous lads responded to their call though they might die for it. It could be the first slip that killed them. Hundreds were lost in ships which went missing off the Horn and no one knows what was their fate. They could sail suddenly by night into ice, be dismasted and the ship's own steel yards flail her to death as she pitched in the sea: be flung on her beam ends, the hatches stove in, and down like a stone. Even in the 20th century, it was not unusual some years for ten or twelve big square-riggers to be missing: they sailed silently and were silent forever after, overwhelmed somehow in the sea.

These apprentices were a fine lot of young fellows of considerable spirit or they would scarcely have gone to sea in sail at all. Many made splendid seamen. For years the best graduates among them were recruited exclusively for all the great British steamship lines – Cunard, White Star, Blue Funnel, Elder Dempster, Shaw Savill, P and O and so on. These companies required their bridge officers to be certificated master-mariners, qualified in sail, before they could be watchkeepers at all. This was so at least until the 1914–1918 war. It was not that they required sailing-ship *knowledge* as such. What they appreciated was the solid basis of sound seamanship and, above all, the calm ability to handle emergencies which the sail-trained young man absorbed. He was a *proven* man.

All in Britain who aspired to serve as merchant-ship officers had to finance their own schooling which could be a greater expense for the young fellow who served his time before the mast, because he came ashore with more to learn. Nobody *had* to be an apprentice. There were a few excellent ships manned almost wholly by cadets (such as Messrs Devitt and Moore's in the Australian trade, the traditions of which are still carried on in the 1970's at the Nautical College at Pangbourne, in England). But the intelligent, industrious and sober A.B. could save from his wages, finance his own schooling (a few weeks of that should suffice) and pass for his certificates, too. This was done by many Welsh, West Country and Scots lads who began in the excellent school of their own small ships.

It was not at all required (nor always sense) that lads should begin in large sailing-ships. A sea-minded boy could begin in any size ship so long as she made deepsea voyages and rated as square-rigged – that is, was at least a brigantine or barquentine, not a coasting ketch or schooner. A brigantine had the standard complete rig of square sails on the foremast, consisting of the course, two topsails, and a topgallant. Some had the luxury (or nuisance) of a royal. The top'sl schooner rig would not pass, for such vessels, carrying only two square tops'ls on the fore and a big fore-and-aft foresail, rated legally as fore-and-afters. British lads had access to a large and efficient fleet of small square-rigged short-voyage ships in the days of sail, mainly brigantines or barquentines in such countries as Wales, Ireland, and Scotland, and the counties of Devon and Cornwall as well. Many seafaring families considered that, for the surer foundation of their knowledge, their sons should start in smaller ships such as these and graduate to the big deepwatermen when they were well grounded in their business and strong enough to survive in it. One thinks that these were right. Probably at least three-fourths of the premium apprentices recruited in England came from families with little or no connection with the sea, though this would appear not to have affected their aptitude at all once they settled down.

Crews of deepsea square-riggers were international, especially from about 1880 to the end of the era and particularly in British and American deepwatermen. The masters and officers were usually of the same nationality as their ships, in some countries (particularly France) by law. By and large the landless, the non-inheritors, the under-privileged anywhere from Tasmania to Newfoundland, Scotland to Scandinavia and North Germany, Cornwall and all Wales to the coasts of Portugal – these took to the sometimes harsh, always challenging and at times dangerous life of the deepwater sailing-ships' sea, and served it magnificently. In a man's real fulfillment, the sailing-ship also served them well. For century after century through at least a thousand years (disregarding the ships and mariners of the East) she did all man's carriage by sea, and the fighting too. She did it magnificently though perhaps with high casualties. She used up no resources and consumed nothing she did not carry with her. She offered men a challenging but deeply satisfying life without nervous stress, but with instead the deep satisfaction of the exercise of a splendid natural skill.

For the sailing-ship performed her share of the world's

work by grace of man's patiently acquired, long nurtured skills – his use of plain aerofoils called sails set from spars on high masts to convert the understood ocean winds into successful long voyages. These ships sailed in peace under God, silently, with grace. They destroyed nothing except occasionally themselves, for the price of error was high. They polluted nothing. They made all the great voyages of discovery. They opened up the earth, and they shifted peoples.

Now a heedless generation has thrown these great ships and those skills away. A few powered auxiliaries, though better than nothing, will not restore them nor the knowledge of handling and voyage-making in them. Nor will books.

II

Ship-handling under sail

SHIP-handling means inducing a vessel to do what she must, and to go where she has to go, in safety, without waste of resources or of time. Here as elsewhere in this book one speaks of sail, but the basic principles apply also to powered ships. Square-riggers might have individual idiosyncracies or even built-in imperfections (poor centre of effort, wrong spacing of masts, clumsy hulls). But the essential manoeuvres were much the same in all, from a Maldivian brig or the replica *Mayflower* to the giant four-masted barque, steel to her trucks and well over 300 feet on her waterline length.

It did not take long for any bright lad to learn the ropes, literally. He lived in his ship day and night. She was forever in his sight and, very often, nothing else was. He was surrounded by tough able seamen led by officers equally tough, all setting higher standards in the daily performance of their work than the most exacting surgical sister did in hers, for both knew that a slip could kill someone; for the seaman, that someone could be himself. There was a great deal of heavy gear above their heads and something not properly secured could fall down at any swift change of over-strong wind. A fool at the wheel could cause the ship to be caught aback, which was to let the wind get on the front of the square sails instead of blowing always at some useful angle into them from behind. Or, when running in heavy seas, he could let her broach-to, which was to fall into the trough of the sea where she was temporarily unmanageable.

The first thing a new cadet, or apprentice, or deck-boy did on joining if he had any sense (if he had not, then he would quickly develop some) was to learn his ship's gear and way of doing things, from the belaying-pin pattern to the best

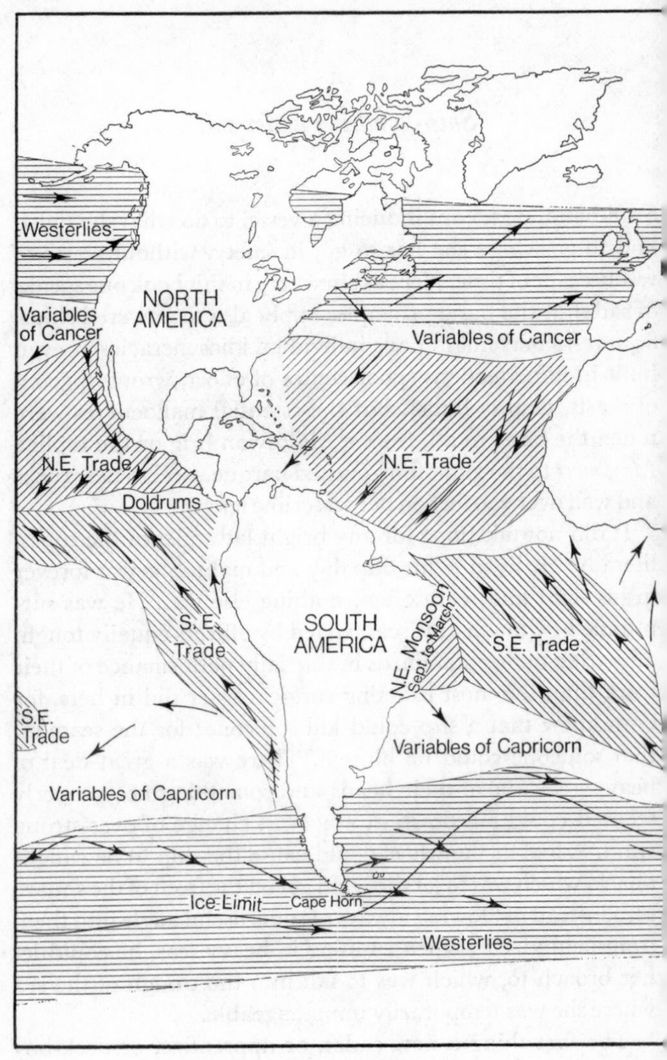

Map of the world showing the Ocean Winds.

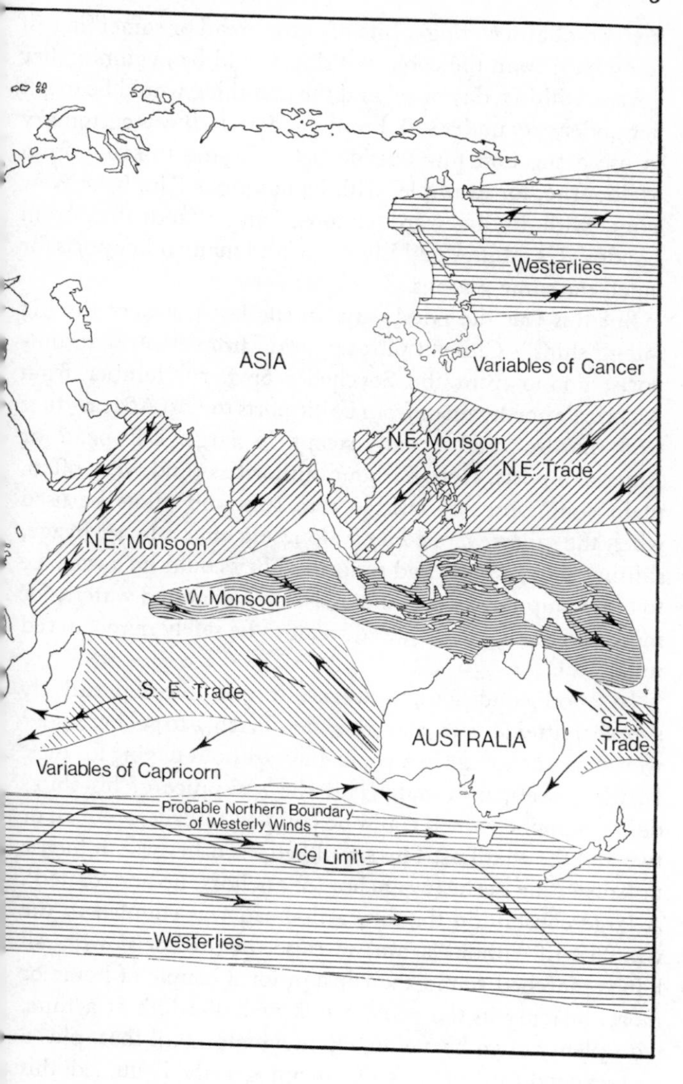
Westerlies
ASIA
Variables of Cancer
N.E. Monsoon
N.E. Trade
N.E. Monsoon
W. Monsoon
S. E. Trade
S.E. Trade
AUSTRALIA
Variables of Capricorn
Probable Northern Boundary of Westerly Winds
Ice Limit
Westerlies

method of abstracting a bite of extra bread or something (if to be had) from the cook. His ship would be beginning her voyage within a day or so, and the first thing would be to get her under way under sail. From some ports, it was customary to use a tug and tow outside before trying to sail – from Melbourne, for example, with its notorious Rip, from New York, with its awkward channels and vast traffic, from London, Hamburg, and Liverpool and many other ports for much the same reasons.

But this was the boys' way. In the last trades of the big sailing ships – Chilean nitrates, grain from Australian outports, guano from the Seychelles or Peru, lumber from America's northwest or from Baltic ports to East Africa – tugs were hardly used at all except in large European or American ports. Here harbour authorities (and, very often, plain commonsense) insisted that tugs and pilots be used when the sailers were coming alongside after a long voyage, shifting ship in port, and so forth. They could be a menace to other shipping and to themselves in congested waters, for most square-riggers required room to be safely manoeuvred under sail.

In good conditions, however, it was a comparatively simple matter for a master who knew his ship to get her under way from anchorage in an open bay, without paying for tugs. In big vessels, he usually had the assistance of his ship's donkey-engine, which could be coupled to drive a winch or two and the windlass. This simplified the otherwise immense task of getting the heavy anchor (or anchors) up and 'catted'. A large capstan on the forecastle-head was coupled to the windlass (if without steam) to raise the anchor slowly. All hands marched round the capstan for a couple of hours or more, heaving in the cable a link or half-a-link at a time, with plenty of yo-heave-ho, chanteying and all that, plus a vast expenditure of muscle. Steam greatly lightened this heavy job, but the anchor when broken out had still to be brought to the surface, 'fished' and 'catted' – that is, have

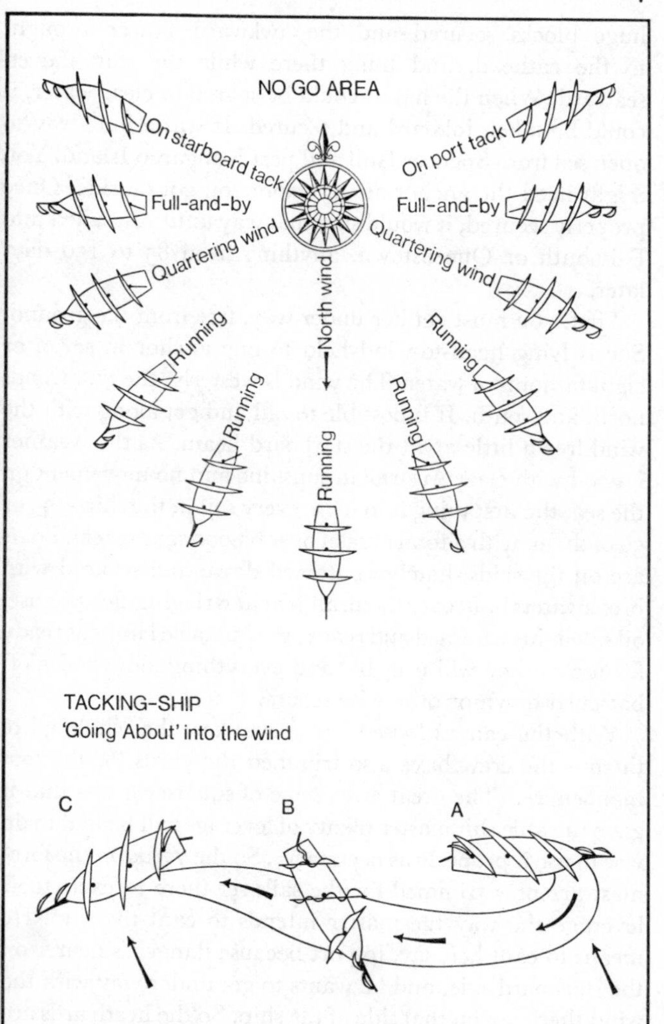
NO GO AREA
On starboard tack
On port tack
Full-and-by
Full-and-by
Quartering wind
Quartering wind
North wind
Running
Running
Running
Running
Running
Running
TACKING-SHIP
'Going About' into the wind
C
B
A

huge blocks secured and the awkward bower brought to the cathead, and hung there while the ship moved seaward. When the hands could be spared in clear water, it could be taken inboard and secured. It was a long way to open sea from Spencer Gulf and past Kangaroo Island. You might need the anchor again before you got outside. Once properly secured, it would stay that way until you sailed into Falmouth or Queenstown, anything from 85 to 150 days later.

First, you must get her under way, free from the ground. She is lying head-to-wind held to one anchor in seven or eight fathoms of water. The wind is westerly, the gulf trends north and south. It is possible to sail and get along with the wind free a little abaft the starboard beam. As the weather is good with clear Australian sunshine and no movement on the sea, the first thing is to loose every sail in the ship – 35 or 36 of them, with a total area of over 65,000 square feet. Boats are on the skids, hatches battened down and secured with breakwaters built over them, all gear and rigging clear for use, oil sidelights trimmed and ready, the binnacle lamps as ready for use as they will ever be, and everything alow and aloft battened down or otherwise secure.

With the canvas loosed – jibs, spanker, the whole 36 of them – the crew have also trimmed the yards for the first manoeuvre. (The great advantage of square rig was that it gave the able shipmaster plenty of leverage; all he had to do was to use it properly as necessary). So the yards on the foremast are now trimmed for the sails set there to exert their leverage the way the master intends to cant the ship. He means to cant her, say, to port because danger is nearer on the starboard side, and he wants to get under way with the wind therefore on that side of the ship. So the headyards are braced round to port, the main and mizzen to starboard. They are all aback while the anchor holds the ship into the wind. With the ship brought almost but not quite above her anchor – 'up and down' was the term – the crew now run to set some square sail on all three square-rigged masts, usually the six topsails first. The big ship gets restless, like a race-horse being saddled in its stall. She tugs at her anchor and shifts her head restlessly a few points, while the wind begins to sigh in the rigging. So far to go! So much work to be done! (The ship has not sufficient man-power to handle the sails and the heavy cable and anchor at the same time, for that anchor has to be brought right aboard, secure upon the fore-castle-head before the ship begins her endless motion in the open sea. Those great steel yards aloft are heavy, too, and there is no power but 'Armstrong's patent' for handling them).

The sails are set by sheeting the lower topsails first (meaning that the lower corners are hauled downwards and out to the yardarms immediately below them, in this case the course yards: these sheets are of heavy chain and their hauling ends reach to the deck) and then stretching the upper tops'ls. Their sheets reach to the deck too, generally, but are left fast: the sail is stretched upwards by hoisting its yard until the canvas is taut, ready for work. The six tops'ls give sufficient working canvas to get the ship away: set courses would merely be an inconvenience until she is free of the ground and on her voyage. They are loose and ready. So are the spanker (a good fore-and-aft steering sail on the jigger-mast aft) the stays'ls between the masts and the jibs on the bowsprit.

'Up and down!' shouts the Mate, meaning the anchor is just below the bow. 'Break out the anchor! Set the headsails, sheets to starboard!' the Captain shouts: 'A hand to the wheel!' The steward has been standing-by. Now an A.B. rushes aft and takes over, standing on the windward side of the six-foot wheel. The last few links of cable grind reluctantly in.

With the ship free of her anchor, slowly at first and then swiftly, the two fore topsails and the jibs now being aback to accept the wind's pressure from the starboard side, begin to cant her head to port. As she swings, the backed headsails also helping, the wind comes behind the square sails now set on main and mizzenmasts. Having twice as much sail area there, the ship begins to gather way and go ahead.

'Haul round the fore yards! Shift over the jibs!'

Now the sails on the fore also fill. The ship gathers more way and is manageable. The yards and sails are properly trimmed. The anchor is brought up to the hawse. Sail after sail is piled on the ship as rapidly as possible. Lower topsails and lower topgallantsails are sheeted downwards, which means that their lower clews (corners) are stretched towards the extremities of the yards immediately below each of them, by means of heavy iron chains, often led to tackles on deck to help the manpower. Upper topsails and upper topgallants (as well as royals) are set by hauling out their lower corners by wire or wire-and-chain sheets towards the yardarms immediately below them, and then the upper yards are hauled up as far as they will go. This is done by the halliards – literally, haul-yards – led to tackles on deck. Same process with the royals. Boys race aloft to slack up anything such as the sails' own handling gear (buntlines, leechlines) which could impede this process – one boy to each square-rigged mast. All know their work, having served in the ship from Europe.

The wind freshens. The ship lists, heels, sings along, comes to life. She is lying up to the wind nicely, a point or two free. She makes six knots, seven, eight. The big courses are set from the deck with wire tacks and sheets led each directly to its own capstan, of which the ship has seven.

Now with all sail set and the beautiful four-master bounding along, the anchor is lifted with the cat and fish tackles, and cockbilled for the time being on the forecastle-head, ready for letting go if necessary. Both big bowers are left like that until the ship is quite clear of the land. Only then the cables will be unshackled and sent below, and the hawse-pipes blocked against the inrush of water as the ship lunges and dives along the road towards the Horn.

All this is only achieved by immense toil. Everyone is fit, strong, willing, for in these last ships food and treatment were generally excellent by earlier standards, though pay was worse than ever and some among the Finns – really Åland Islanders – were not always well manned. A handful of A.B.'s, a brace of Ordinary Seamen and ten or twelve 'teen-aged apprentices – average age 18 at the most – were often the lot, with good tradesmen (carpenter, sailmaker, steward, cook), three excellent young mates, and – this above all – an experienced and thoroughy competent master aged anything from 24 to (in a very few cases) 65 or 70. Most of these men, like many of the Britishers, had been professionally at sea since childhood, beginning as combination second cooks and deck-boys at the age of eight or nine on summer Baltic runs in hard-bitten Ålands schooners. (There were no first cooks in those tough ships.)

In many of those last four-masters the Jarvis brace-winches helped to lighten the work, and that donkey was also a God-send on sailing day when crews were sometimes more than fully extended. It could be different in the heyday of the gaunt Lime-juicers.* For sheer hard work in one enormous and continuous dose, sailing-day in a large, under-manned four-masted barque would take some beating. Perhaps it could be worse only in a ship where poor food and treatment bred resentment, no matter how well-manned.

Now the ship is foaming along in a flat sea under the protection of Kangaroo Island: but she has not really begun her gruelling long voyage until she is outside where the seas heave and break and fling their crests and spray aboard, at times above the course yards. Soon they follow with walls of water, and the main deck is awash feet deep all along the lee side, and the wheel is heavy and the wind roars in all the rigging. Let her go! It is only 15,000 miles or so, with luck. Get her south first, south of Tasmania, to race across the

* For conditions in some of these, see *The War with Cape Horn*, Hodder and Stoughton, London, and Pan Books. Charles Scribner's Sons, New York.

Tasman Sea, south of New Zealand and down towards the ice-line's northern rim – let her go! For this is Roaring Forties, Shrieking Fifties, Snarling Sixties sailing, with gale after gale marching in noisy procession across the bottom of the world and your great ship flung along in a roaring wet tumult of gale and sea at speed towards Cape Horn.

Or so you hope. It was rarely as easy as that. Good sailing winds do not appear to order. I have been 30 days from Port Victoria (well inside Spencers Gulf in S. Australia) to past the Horn, in the four-masted barque *Parma* in 1933, and 57 days from Wallaroo (also up the Gulf) in the ship *Grace Harwar*, in 1929. In that ship we were driven away from the south of New Zealand by a south-easterly gale, and had to beat through Cook Straits. So it goes. I was with de Cloux once in the *Herzogin Cecilie* (in 1928) when he had to beat through Bass Straits, a rough spot well littered with islands.

You may well have to beat – which means to tack against a head wind which will not allow the square-rigger to lie-up to, or make her course, when she must slog along into it zig-zagging, braced up first on one tack, then the other – before you get the ship clear of Spencer's Gulf or Kangaroo Island. To tack, you have to throw the ship aback and across the wind in its face, which can be rough going in the square-rigger where the masts are stayed for the wind's pressure *behind* the sails, not in front of them. You can – indeed, you must when the wind is very strong and to tack might cause damage – put the ship round by 'wearing' her. Then you run her off, keeping the wind *in* the sails by manipulating helm and braces, never in front of them, while you make a horse-shoe bend swinging the yards right round until you have brought her up to the wind again ahead of the other beam. This, obviously, can waste hard-won ground, sometimes a lot. There were some slovenly or fat-bellied ships that would not tack at all and so always had to be put about by wearing. These made long passages and were avoided if possible.

Tacking square-riggers was a nice exercise in expert sea-

The German-built 4-masted barque, *Herzogin Cecilie* (above), was sold to Finland where she was employed in the Australian trade. Below, she races for Cape Horn, on a voyage in 1928. A deck view looking aft.

Cape Horn was easier to pass in summer. We sometimes sighted it.

The 5-masted ship *Preussen*, the only such ship built.

Plenty of water about the main deck in bad weather near Cape Horn.

manship at any time – a rather different matter from the same thing in fore-and-aft rigged vessels. The old seamen's manuals, guides for examinations and so forth were all very well for those who knew their work properly at first hand. You needed skill and good judgement or you could make an awful botch of any manoeuvre in a square-rigger. You couldn't learn the realities of such things in books, or study how to keep your nerve.

Well, just how would you 'tack ship'? Nicholls' *Seamanship* (and Viva Voce Guide) was still asking the question as late as 1918, and provided a brief answer:

> See all clear for going about, keep the ship clean full, and station the hands. When ready, put the *Helm a-lee,** ease off or let go the head and fore sheets, and haul the spanker boom amidships. When from 1 to 2 points from head to wind, *Mainsail Haul.** Haul the head sheets over when the wind gets on the other bow, and ease off the spanker boom. When filling aft, *Fore Bowline Let go and Haul,** and train (trim) all sail for the other tack.

It is all there, perhaps, if you are thoroughly familiar with the operation already. But that account is just what it is meant to be, an answer for a verbal examination, to be gabbled off and on to the next. These old seamanship 'Guides', after all, were no record for posterity but meant for the one purpose, to help get knowledgeable candidates through what they considered the formidable examinations for their Board of Trade certificates of competence, without which there was no advancement in the profession. It was usual for aspiring candidates to have Nicholls (or Reids, or some-such) along with them in the forecastle or half-deck. They knew the *jobs* only too well: all they needed were the *words*. (One might add, after one swift look and a few words, his examiner knew his *candidate*, too. He could soon fail the occasional fool, no matter how glib.)

To tack a real square-rigger, unless the conditions were excellent – with a fine sailing breeze, no sea running to speak

* These were the standard orders as used in British ships.

of, plenty of sea-room, a competent, contented and sufficient crew – could be a great deal of work at best and an awful mess at an easily attained worst. What you had to do was to swing the ship across the wind – get everything aback for a moment or two (maybe longer) as she swung, without picking up sternway or (what was worse) getting the ship in such a jam that she would not cant either way. Then you had to handle her with sternway, losing miles. Some of the more modern, rather brutish type of ships were very difficult to tack at all – the wall-sided stumpy-rigged waggons with badly-spaced masts and poor centre of effort, and bows so blunt they pushed half the sea before them (instead of slipping along so smoothly that all the hull followed without realising it was being moved at all), and sterns that dragged the other half behind. It was not their elephantine hulls alone that caused this cussedness but the placing of their masts, or any mess-up of the centre of effort of the sails. There were art, science, *flair* in square-rigger design: or should be. If you are going to ask a 3,000-ton ship not just to survive in full storms but to race under control through them and keep it up perhaps for week after week, and to beat to wind'ard in half a gale when required, then she must not be a wall-sided, bitchy, bad-tempered tub. But some were. Others could be made so in the hands of an incompetent master or a bloody-minded crew.

You did your best. Generally you won though often a lad or two went overboard – at times, two or three together; on some terrible occasions, a whole watch. This could happen when they were at the ship's side, trying to square her in by the old style long braces, and she rolled down more than she should just as the crest of a particularly savage breaker rose above her. Then it broke aboard, pinning the side down for some terrible moments – the wind screaming, sea roaring. When she lifted that side again, nobody was there.

Sailing-ships *were* dangerous. You had to be careful how you handled them. To play safe in bad weather or to lessen the risk of damage, you could change tacks by 'wearing' the ship round instead of tacking her. Obviously, you lost more ground that way and she could roll her guts out, too, before the wind, filling the maindeck perhaps dangerously with water – swirling, snarling, man-killing water in which the crew had to work. They could be knocked down with swift and fatal ease, and rolled overboard.

Well, they knew that, and watched for it. No man was his brother's keeper . . . As a general rule, the tack-ship manoeuvre was practical only in relatively fine weather.

The essence of watch-keeping was strict and continuous attention to the trim of the yards and the set of the sails, of which a sufficiency was set at any and all times to get the best speed from the ship in the prevailing conditions – a sufficiency, and no more, for more was strain and strain was damage.

The master and his watch-keeping mates – first and second – watched like hawks for sign of changing wind, of coming alterations of force or direction. Either could come suddenly down there in the Roaring Forties and Shrieking Fifties. There were signs: you had better notice them.

In the Australian trade, after all, you were lucky: you had only to stay clear of the land, run for your life to get round Cape Horn, swing to the left and keep on going another eight or nine thousand miles before threading her into the English Channel. It was the *other* way, *beating* not running, that was truly rugged especially in the long dark winters. That was the tough stuff. But that route, the great highway for the Chilean nitrate trader and ships bound for Peru, Santa Rosalia, Puget Sound or California, was little used after the Panama Canal was opened. From the seaman's point of view, perhaps this was just as well: but for the long period when it offered the only way westwards from the S. Atlantic to the Pacific, square-riggers great and small, from the little Welsh copper-ore barques to the great five-masters *Potosi* and *Preussen*, the softwood Yankee clippers to the beautiful Scots iron square-rigged masterpieces and the hungry Lime-juicers, took it on by the hundreds.

And they mostly won though not without losses, no matter how well they were sailed. In the one year 1905 alone, 55 ocean-going ships were posted missing at Lloyds in London, which means that each began a normal voyage in some port or other and none ever arrived anywhere, not the ships nor a single man of the 2,000-or-so who manned them. Thirty-two of these ships were British, 14 of them on Cape Horn voyages – among them the well-known *Glenburn*, *Principality*, *Bay of Bengal*, *Alcinous*, each gone in eternal silence with her half-deck full of apprentices and everybody else aboard. There was much ice reported that southern winter – much ice, and the usual savage gales.

III

Passage making

A 'PASSAGE', in the days of sail, meant a run from one port to another, in ballast or laden. A 'voyage' was a round trip, a passage out and a passage back: but the words were both at times used loosely. The big British, German, American and French ships made many strange peregrinations round the earth, while they lasted. Any voyage however long (the British crew agreements allowed for three years) was a series of passages, all more or less familiar to the experienced master. U.K./Continent to Australia or California, or to almost anywhere on the west coast of South America were commonplace first legs, and, sooner or later, back to U.K./Continent from almost anywhere with some bulk cargo that was hard to find and slow to load. Such cargoes included guano from remote Peruvian islands, nitrates from Chile that set like rock, grain from California or an Australian outport, or lumber from British Columbia or Puget Sound.

The general pattern was that the sailer must content herself with cargoes that were slow to load or in the more difficult and less accessible ports, or both. Not even the cheapest old steam tramp could really afford to anchor off a Peruvian (or an Indian Ocean) island while a cargo of accumulated bird droppings (called guano) was scraped off the rocks and ferried out to her by the boatload. This process could take months. Bunker coal, engine-room stores, safe berthing facilities, good boiler water were the steamships' minimum demands. Nor could she afford to wait months for a grain harvest to ripen as she swung in expensive idleness in San Francisco Bay or anywhere else. Her overheads were higher than the sailers by far, and – most important – she could be more effectively managed by her owners than any old 'windjammer' could. By the 20th century many of these were owned by small syndicates with minimal capital and little effective management at all.

From anywhere to anywhere else, the square-rigger's passage followed much the same broad pattern – first get away from the land and then stay away, using the west winds zones for making easting, the tradewinds for latitude mainly but for westing, too, if bound to the westward across the N. Atlantic, the Indian, or the N. or S. Pacific Oceans. As for other zones (especially if west-bound north of 40 Deg. N. latitude) she had to slog it out. Masters had to use their own experience, commonsense, and such store of hard-won knowledge as they might have had handed down to them or built up for themselves. There were books, some of them good, and – later – wind and weather charts of some approximation but much better than nothing. The Germans had the best books dating back to the 1890's, the U.S. Hydrographic Office had the best weather charts (issued monthly), and the Lords Commissioners of the Admiralty, through their hydrographic department, had published an elementary work called Ocean Passages for the World in 1896 and another (somewhat but not much better) edition in 1923. These 'Passages' were little more than hopefully recommended routes, based largely (said My Lords) on the log records furnished by two British lines – J. Hardie & Co., and Thos. Law's *Shires* – whose ships were scarcely to be regarded as 'cracks' of any sort, nor had many of them the reputation of being particularly well sailed. A few had made the occasional good passage. Messrs John Hardie & Co., of Glasgow, provided most of the information in 1914–15 when they had vessels like the four-masted barques *Hougomont*, *Vimeira* and *Archibald Russell*, each of some 2,400 tons, and the barques *Kildalton*, *Killoran* and *Kilmeny*, of 1,700 tons or so, a hard-working fleet or no particular sailing distinction. Thos. Law then had seven large square-riggers, three of them ships and four four-masted barques.

For practical guidance, one found the American pilot-charts and the German *Segelhandbuch** to be the best. Information in the Admiralty tome was very general. The German books were fascinating reading to a sailing-ship sailor, especially when trying to make some of those passages. For example, one read how in 1893, the barque *Atalanta* (1,100 tons, built by Germania-Werft at Kiel in 1886) had sailed from Geelong, Australia, to off the Horn in 29 days, at an average speed of 8½ knots. Any such passage from anywhere in Australia to the Horn in less than a month was remarkable, especially in the later-day big metal square-rigger. The famous 'clippers' in their brief day claimed many shorter passages than that, and made some of them too. The *Atalanta* went on to complete that passage in 83 days from Geelong to the Channel. This was long after the clipper days, and her good run went unnoticed.

As far as one knows, it was only once again equalled when the Finnish (formerly Scots) four-masted barque *Parma* (3,000-plus tons) bringing 5,000 tons of grain from Port Victoria in Spencer Gulf, South Australia, in 1932, was 83 days anchorage to anchorage. She was 30 days from her anchorage off Port Victoria to the Horn, 56 to the Line, 83 to Falmouth. We sailed that year at least five or six hundred miles more than the *Atalanta* had on her 83-day run, for Geelong was that much closer to England.

It wasn't so much the sailing that did it (though Captain de Cloux, who was master, kept her at it day and night all that time) but the not-stopping, and to some degree that may

* My own copies were published in 1897 and 1910 by Deutsche Seewarte, the earlier for the Pacific, the later for the Atlantic. They were in the *Parma* when we bought her in Hamburg in 1932 and were interesting and invaluable. They were aboard as part of the ship's navigation inventory – not a former master's property. The British shipmaster was usually required to furnish his own navigational needs even to the essential charts, though enlightened owners sometimes supplied a set of Findlays Directories, one to each major ocean, usually over a thousand pages and now very interesting. In 1884 the publisher was Richard Holmes Laurie, of 53 Fleet Street, London.

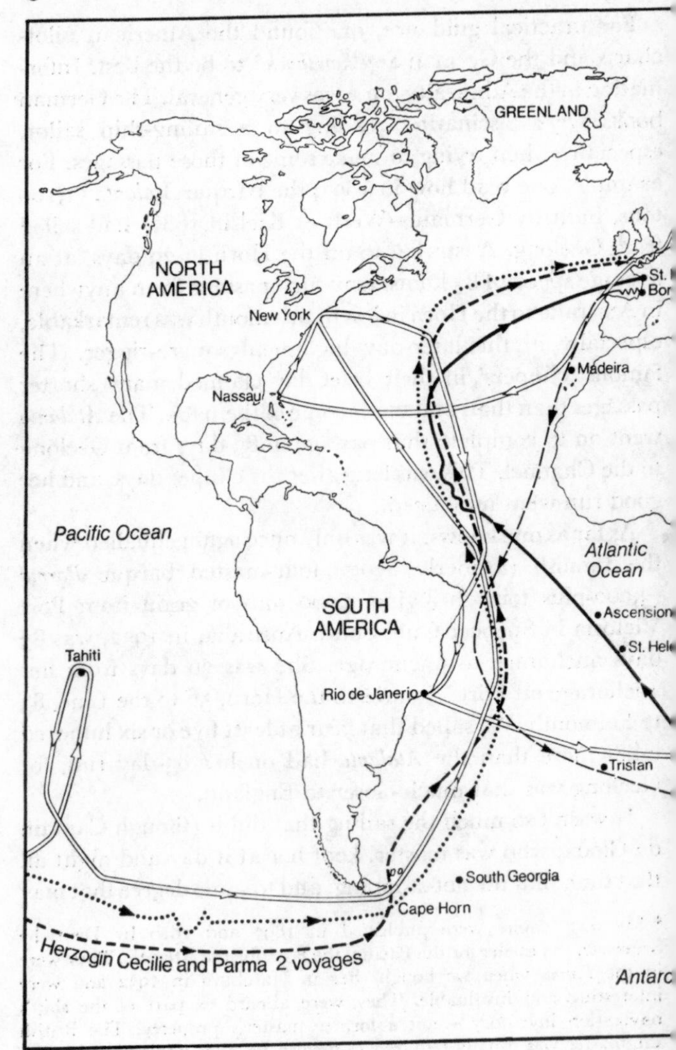

Some sailing-ship voyages made by the author.

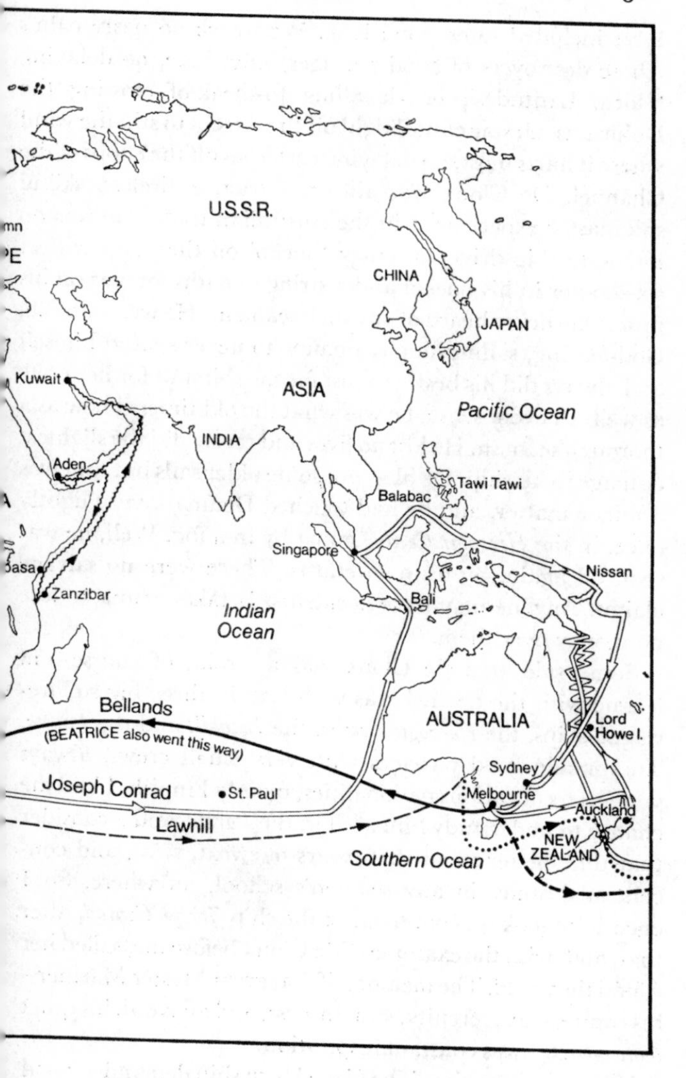
U.S.S.R.
CHINA
JAPAN
ASIA
Kuwait
INDIA
Pacific Ocean
Aden
Tawi Tawi
Balabac
Singapore
Nissan
Zanzibar
Bali
Indian Ocean
Bellands
(BEATRICE also went this way)
AUSTRALIA
Lord Howe I.
Sydney
Joseph Conrad
St. Paul
Melbourne
Auckland
Lawhill
NEW ZEALAND
Southern Ocean

have included some good luck. We struck no nasty calms (those destroyers of good passages) anywhere, no delaying 'Horse Latitudes', no dawdling to-speak-of crossing the Doldrums, no stagnant 'High' off the Azores to still the wind where it hurts most, no delaying easterlies off the chops of the Channel. De Cloux was always a trier, a tireless, skilful shipmaster experienced in the Australian trade. He was no insensate ship-driver, a crazy 'bucko' on the poop with a six-shooter in his pocket and a string of oaths forever on his lips. (One never heard of any such seamen.) He was a simple, God-fearing, sailing-ship seaman who never spared himself and always did his best, not just for the ship but for her crew as well. In every sense, he was what the old timers knew as a thorough seaman. He lost no lives and rarely did the slightest damage to his ship. He blew out some older sails but that was a minor matter, and he had touched Denmark very lightly once, in the *Herzogin Cecilie*, going by in a fog. Well, he was soon off again, by his own efforts. There were no salvage claims. Anyone may have accidents. It takes genius to lose no money over them.

Some said that de Cloux was a 'troll', of course – in league with the devil. I was with him in three big square-rigged ships, the *Herzogin Cecilie*, the *Lawhill* and the *Parma*. They made good passages with very small crews, always youngsters of various nationalities, mainly Finnish. I had the chance to understudy him a bit in the *Parma*, and I consider that time better spent than years of sweat, swot, and concentrated study in any seamen's school, anywhere. So I cheerfully took on command of the ship *Joseph Conrad*, after that, and, with the example of de Cloux before me, sailed her round the world. The memory of that great Master Mariner – his competence, serenity, straightness, and above all his quiet *thoroughness* – was constant inspiration.

He was outstanding. The Cape Horn ship demanded good masters and got them, more often than not. There might be the very occasional tired incompetent and a few drunks.

Some lively old boys were still in command of big ships at surprisingly advanced ages – up to 80-or-so – usually for the rather sad reason that, at £12 or £14 a month, they could not retire. They had gone to sea as younger sons and had little or no inheritance. Many of their wives sailed with them. No one blamed these good old men for, at times, taking things easy. Some died in harness. Most were men in harmony with their ships, whose whole lives and thoughts (in storms above all) were for their ships, and their ships could speak to them in ways no power-driven vessel ever did or could. No throbbing sea-punching propeller thundered behind them, no noisy shaft deadened the sound of wind and sea, no pulsing engines, no clang of fireman's shovel on steel stoke-hold floor, no whining old Wear pump disturbed the natural sounds that were the square-rigger's orchestra – a harmony of wind, ship and sea. The ship herself called any good master when she needed him, and he was up on deck in a bound – on deck and in charge.

For this he also needed perfect night vision. I noted that de Cloux was one of those masters who went to great pains for this. In violent weather his quarters never knew him, for he cat-napped on a makeshift bunk – a sort of fore-and-aft shelf with a board at the side – in the charthouse on the poop. He used no lights: those who called him had instructions to shine no torch, strike no match. To come out on the deck of a big square-rigged ship fighting a wild gale suddenly increasing in the stormy night could be a terrifying experience with its wild orchestra of the mighty roar of the wind, the whiplash of the flying sea-crests over the ship, the scream in all the shrouds and backstays as she rolled shudderingly to wind'ard, and the crash of great seas over the rail – at times, too, the thunder-claps of a blown-out tops'l ripped from yard and bolt-rope in a shrieking, savage squall, and gone in an instant. Who commands must keep his nerve! The *right* action is imperative, instantly, for the snarling crests of gale-mad seas are forever curling high above the poop, threatening murder, and the great ship stretches her assaulted length into the frightening night ahead. No star shines, no moon breaks the blackened heavens, screaming with gale . . . The good Master takes it all in upon the instant. It sounds as if heaven is maddened by the hurricane wind but it is only the normal clamour of the gale. The sleet and whipped-up spume from the crests of the seas hurt the face when you look wind'ard. But keep her going! Keep her going, under God: and you shall aid God and yourself by the care of your good ship all the time, by the spirit you have quietly nourished in your crew all the voyage, too.

With night vision unimpaired you may see at once how things really are, despite the assault of the braggart wind. The blackened shapes of the few sails set lean gloriously to their work, and you can see them – those that should be set *are* set, and pulling uproariously, not with the roar of threat but of organised power. That's the thing! Keep it organised, if not under your full control, at least at your bidding.

You shall *not* heave-to, which is to take the way off her under very short sail, to bring her to the wind and let her lie there like an albatross asleep, until the morning. For this is fair wind driving a powerful, splendid ship. Let her go! To bring her up is to risk damage, for she will fall into the troughs before she shoulders the crests, rolling most violently. To heave-to is to stop her forward speed but not her motion. No, no, no! Let her go! It is not *that* bad.

But your judgement had better be right.

> The Great Southern Ocean, which offers the only direct water-route right round the globe, may be considered as the *main track of sailing-ships*, on account of the strong westerly winds which there prevail, and may be depended upon at all seasons of the year to afford a swift passage, unimpeded by dangers.

So states the British Admiralty '*Ocean Passages for the World*' (1923) with unwarranted optimism and insufficient data. What is all this about swift passages, *no* dangers? Half the summer run from S.E. Australia towards the Horn is inside the ice-line, with more than enough dangerous until islands to get in the way. The winds down there 'screameth as they listeth' and are by no means always fair. Cape Horn is too far south for comfort at any time and in winter is hell. Strong westerly winds reliable? The master must have skill to keep his square-rigged command in the correct semi-circle of all those spiralling cyclonic movements, for it is detailed knowledge of the storm that he needs to maintain his ship's forward speed and day-to-day safety. As the ship races along so also do the vast movements of the wind, very much faster. He must not allow the wind ever to jump ahead of him with force, for his square-rigged masts are set up and stayed to accept stresses in the sails from behind or abeam of them. (The masts cannot be supported from ahead, or the yards could not swing properly at all, for the canvas would be chewed up on them – chafed swiftly to impotence.)

'Running the Easting down' called for constant knowledgeable alertness. Indeed, the only stage of the whole 15,000 mile passage where watchkeepers might relax a little was in the Trade Winds, thousands of miles away. There were years when even the Trades were curiously unsettled, for there was no guarantee of any 'regular' winds, not even them. You are not to imagine that, because you are in the 'right' latitudes, the wind has read the same books. The price of your safety and progress is the constant, wary vigilance of good watch-keeping day and night backed by all the knowledge you can muster, and no dogmatic views on anything. You *will* get notice of coming change. Pressure plots are a help but only a help: a wary eye on the barometer is an elementary precaution.

'First rise after Low
Foretells stronger blow'*

* These odd ditties were pretty sound, like:
'With rising wind and falling glass
Soundly sleeps the silly ass'.

The gale 'bloweth as it listeth', indeed, but over thousands of miles of open ocean, it obeys the rules. As well as that upwards flick of the mercury, there will quickly be a clearing in the clouded sky away on the lee quarter, followed (often very rapidly) by a leap of the gale to full storm and simultaneous switch of direction through eight or ten compass points, from NNW through W to SW, or SSW, blowing even harder and shrieking in the rigging as if with insane delight. 'I've got you now! *Now* I can tear the masts out, smash in the hatches, let the sea in! Damn you, sink!' So you easily could, the ship gone down in her stride without a chance to send a signal (had she the means), clear away a boat or as much as a plank.

This sort of thing and variants happened to us at least a dozen times on that 30-day rush by the *Parma* from Port Victoria to Cape Horn in '33. We didn't sink. One good reason was that, for all its ferocity, that jump of the wind gave clear warning of its intention. The officers of the watch were ready. The big four-master was already well shortened down, minimal canvas hurling her onwards in the night, watchful A.B.'s or senior cadets at the wheel (aged 17 or 18) the best of watch-keeping officers in their early 20's standing to wind'ard beside the Master, alert, ready, used to this kind of thing and knowing the signs, though they sail for the Horn only once yearly. (Running the Easting down south of Good Hope offered the same conditions, and winter sailing in the North Atlantic could be worse.) They know the ship – her strength, her idiosyncracies, occasional bitchiness and all.

They swing the yards to take the wind on the other quarter, see to the sheeting of the fore course without letting any of the gear take charge, shift over the sheets of the fore topmast staysail. The lower tops'ls will take care of themselves with a little bracing. Nothing else is set, for she is making maximum speed. To over-drive at her best speed is only to strain the ship. Let her go! Turns at the weather side of the wheel are an hour only. It is enough, for he who stands there is in immediate charge and it is heavy, *very* heavy.

Let her go, it is. That passage we were 30 days (from the anchorage well inside Spencers Gulf) to abeam of the Horn.

That was a splendid beginning, but it was only the beginning of that long run. There were plenty of chances of serious delay in the Atlantic, north and south. We still had some 9,000 miles to go. You don't just swing round to the left and keep on going all that way. The greatest enemy then can well be not wind but its absence, for there were several notorious zones of calms and baffling winds to be sailed through – the north and south 'Horse Latitudes' and the Doldrums, the worst of them – before we could hope for a landfall on the British Isles. One was always grateful, too, that we were making for Falmouth Bay and not further into the English Channel, for the risk of some blundering steamer bashing into us there could be worse than the risks on the run for the Horn.

IV

Round the Horn

In the old days and, indeed, until the Panama Canal was successfully built, fair winds summer sailing round Cape Horn scarcely was reckoned a real Horn rounding at all. That rating was kept for westwards passages, *against* the prevailing winds, preferably not in summer, for that season could offer pleasant periods of weather even down there. It was the savage slog against the westerlies in the short and sullen winter days that was the supreme effort, the 'uphill' way. That was the ship-killer, the searching test of ships, shipmasters and their men – the windward thrash through Drake's Passage (Drake had found it by summer: until then the only way to the west was through the Straits of Magellan whose hazards were obvious). Drake's Passage was wide and, for larger ships, greatly preferable to Magellan's Straits. Drake would doubtless have used it had he known of its existence before being blown back that way after reaching the Pacific through the Straits, but the tradition then was of an endless Tierra del Fuego joined to Antarctica.

Ice was a risk, of course, but not usually a great one. It seemed to vary year by year. A good many ships went missing on Cape Horn voyages, probably in the old days something between 12 and 20 a year. Because they were missing the causes of their actual fate remain unknown, for they simply sailed in silence and never came in from the sea at all. (Even in the 1970's steamships and motor-ships still do that, but in some cases it could now be that their own cargoes are more dangerous than the sea.)

'Posted Missing' is a finality of almost absolute mystery. No ship the fate of which has ever become known is on that grim list, and the inquiries are lengthy, thorough and world-

A roaring sea threatens to break over the ship *Joseph Conrad*, but she will lift to it. No such sea broke over the stern, even in a winter rounding of the Horn (above). It looks easy enough to keep upright when the decks are awash (below), but the ship herself is rolling heavily – note the convenient lifelines.

You need footropes of strong wire for this kind of work! A heavy wind tries to lash the seamen's oilskins from their backs.

wide. It was not so much storms which took those ships but bashing into ice or the iron-bound, merciless land – hitting it and, fatally damaged, bouncing off again to sink or capsize and go down like a big stone, with no chance to clear away a boat and no hope of getting anywhere if you did.

But some of the very best of the last big sailing-ships were posted missing, too, among them two school-ships full of boys. (There were those who held that such ships might be especially vulnerable.)

The prime concern of the sailing-ship master was the sailing of his ship, in safety and if possible with speed. He had no 'over-drive'. A square-rigged ship had her best speed and she needed only as much canvas set as would keep her going at that speed: any extra would merely smash seas on board and perhaps strain her. Something then would have to go, some sails at least, and no Bollocky Bill the Sailor, Two-Gun Pete, or Bucko Anybody swaggering on the poop would make any difference except to add to the dangers.

Well, this is all an academic matter now, in the 1970's, for the only craft that sail are a very few auxiliary school-ships and some yachts. Ocean-going yachts have been developed in the 1970's to splendid vessels of proven worth for what they are. The best certainly serve the purpose of providing a red-blooded challenge to red-blooded men. But so does a mountain, provided free by God, cheaper to use and somewhat longer lived. One suggests that circumnavigating yachts are best advised to use the Straits westbound, or Panama Canal preferably, and continue westwards in the tropic zone round the world with favouring winds and currents, dry bunks and warmth. (This is what I would do, if I had a yacht. But they make me sea-sick very easily.)

We were always pleased when we left the Horn behind, even in a 3,000-ton, massively-rigged ship. Indeed, some ships went from S. Australia to the Atlantic the other way, round Good Hope, crossing the Indian Ocean with a fair wind in the trade winds belt and helped past Good Hope by the Agulhas current. One heard of a four-masted barque, the Swedish *C.B. Pedersen* which, thwarted when trying to reach the Indian Ocean south-about from Australia, turned the other way, sailed northwards along the whole east coast of that Commonwealth and thence past the north coast as well, using Torres Strait. This was never recommended except perhaps for ships bound for Mauritius, like Captain Conrad once in the little barque *Otago*, from Sydney, NSW.

On that 83-day run in our *Parma* in 1933, the wind headed us when we were clear of the Horn. The passage thence to the English Channel was no mere turning to the left, hoping for the best, and keeping on going. The golden rule was to do your best with the winds you got, not to moan about your 'bad luck' in not finding better. Making miles mattered more than precise course-keeping, always (so long as you weren't being forced into danger). Pressing the ship into the wind's eye for the sake of compass course made no sense at all for square-riggers. From the Horn to Falmouth Bay, it was obvious that one must make a lot of northing. So with a south-west wind we let her go a bit free on the starboard tack, and sailed on to the westward of the Falkland Islands. We were well off the land, and there was a long way to go before we had much hope of finding the trade winds. The current was with us there by the Falklands, not far out from the Argentine coast. We made in a general way towards the zone of the south-east trade winds.

Here the information on the pilot charts of the Hydrographic Office of the U.S. Navy Dept.* was valuable. It did not bring wind when we had little or none, but it indicated the best course to shape with the winds we found, the area with greatest expectation of reaching the SE Trades with minimal Horse Latitudes, the limits beyond which icebergs had not been reported and that sort of useful information. These charts were "founded upon the researches made in

* Under a U.S. legislative Act of June 1910.

the early part of the 19th century by Matthew Fontaine Maury, while serving as a lieutenant in the U.S. Navy", as each copy reminded us. They were very useful. So were the old Findlay's Ocean Directories, and the excellent German *Segelhandbuch* for the Atlantic Ocean. This was pure sailing-ship stuff methodically collected by sailing-ship people.

As for the worthy Lt. Maury who is often credited with perhaps more than he did, he was certainly a pioneer in trying to collect, classify, and use ocean winds information. One recalls the views of certain hard-headed old 'Down-East' ship-masters that Maury had really found what the masters already knew from their experience and did, then told them with many words to continue to do it. There is no doubt that smart New England shipmasters knew as well as anyone how to drive a ship and where. There is equally no doubt that the '*Physical Geography of The Sea And Its Meteorology*', published by Sampson Low, Son and Marston at 14 Ludgate Hill in London in 1864*, is a classic, and was revolutionary at any rate to some of its readers.

Of course there were no golden rules. There never are. Just as on the run towards the Horn, alert, competent vigilance was the 'guts' of it – incessant, watchful care of your ship, ready at all times to cope with emergencies, watchful alike of shifts of wind and the signs that foretold such things, gauging the strength of the rising wind, weighing up the chances of finding some when there was little or none. You must get the best out of your ship all the time, but you must avoid accidents, costly loss of gear, undue risk to men and boys who accepted enough in the daily round. Day and night, week after week, often month after month, the decisions are yours. Shorten down in time! But when was it time? Only you can say and you know very well that neither you nor anyone else can go on knowing half the answers. You stood there on the reeling poop of the driven ship under

* My copy. Maury's introduction is dated from No. 1 Albemarle Street, London, in November 1860.

God, and you knew it. But drifting into some fool calm zone could be the greater enemy, at any rate in the delay of your ship – perhaps, too, the trial of yourself. One has seen masters jump upon their hats on their own tidy poops, or rush upon a brace-whip or a vang and bite at it. Patience! Patience – that is the thing, too. You must not appear as ass or madman before your crew. Get on meantime with a spot of fishing (you might catch a shark) or clear out the chart-room drawers, make a model, do something! The sailing breeze will come.

Getting through the S. Atlantic, as good a spot to make for as any was about midway between Fernando Noronha off the bulge of Brazil, and the Cape Verde Islands. This gave, as a rule, better trade winds, a clear ocean, and few powered vessels' tracks to cross. It also kept you away from the influence of the Brazil Current which sweeps south along the east coast of Brazil, and a fair chance of working through the Doldrums fast. All such factors helped, though no current was a river in the sea, and all seemed to work much harder against you than they ever did for you. Calm, catspaws, and Doldrums williwaws could be greater hindrances. You must watch those stagnant areas of high pressure in both North and South Atlantics, for these were the real ship-stoppers. But how do you avoid them? Well, the rule was to use the wind you have to blow you where more is, not where it isn't. Watch your barometer and the clouds. Don't get stuck in a 'High'. The crew and the ship may take a bit of a rest now and again. Let her loll there quietly in the sunshine enjoying her reflection in the water for a day or two. You couldn't start her up yourself, anyway. The master may have a day off, too, now and then. Having done your best, sit back and enjoy it. Some masters tickled the bole of the mainmast – a very odd idea – or threw any spare coins they had over the side into the direction from which they sought the wind, 'buying' some from Neptune.

As for that, no sea wind may be regarded as really constant

in either force or direction. You do your best, warily. There was no guarantee of any certainty, though there were a very few shipmasters who seemed able to find good winds at times and places where others could not. One such was the German Captain Hilgendorf of the Hamburg 'P' Line of nitrate traders, who consistently made good passages both ways round the Horn on voyages between Hamburg and Chile – *documented* voyages: no hindsight 'bull' – steadily over the 20-year period between 1881 and 1901 when, at the age of 50, he retired. Over all this time, averaging two

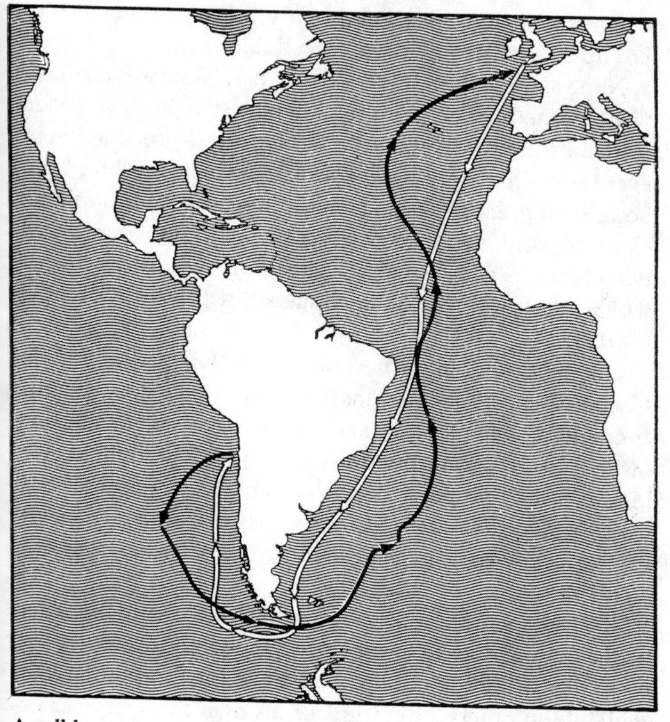

A well-known voyage of the days of sail – outwards to and homewards from Chile by way of Cape Horn. These are the tracks of the famous 5-masted *Potosi*, on a 1912 voyage.

Chilean voyages a year, each meaning both a westwards and eastwards Horn rounding and twice sailing the whole length and breadth of the Atlantic Ocean, he sailed a series of large square-rigged ships – nine in all from the medium-sized *Parsifal* to the great five-masted *Potosi*, from 650 tons to 4,000 – at an *average* speed throughout their voyages under sail alone of 7½ knots. This is a documented and amazing record, never equalled. On 18 such voyages, his average passage between the Channel and his destination in Chile (usually Valparaiso) was 64 days, his average from nitrate ports further north back to Europe was 74 days. This is the best documented and most consistently brilliant sailing record put up by a master of square-rigged ships *ever*.

None of these ships was called clipper. None was especially well-manned. Even the great five-masted barque *Potosi* – probably the best large ocean-going wind-propelled vessel ever built – had only 20 A.B.'s and a crew of 44 all told. The occasional great performances of the pampered, publicised clippers (British or American) in their brief racing lives do not compare with Robert Hilgendorf's consistent record, which is not to belittle the clippers but to give Hilgendorf his due.

One must add, in fairness to all, that Hilgendorf had one tremendous asset denied most others – he had consistently competent, experienced and generous owners, the *same* owners, in all those ships on all his voyages. They appreciated him and they properly rewarded him. They also saw consistently that their ships were properly maintained in every respect, while they owned them. This is a tremendous help on all voyages.

Masters who knew him have told me that Hilgendorf really seemed able to foresee what the wind would do, and profit accordingly: but he had no data other than that available to others – the fruits of his own thought-over experience, and indefatigable pursuit of his overall aim which was to get the best possible performance at all times out of good square-rigged ships. And, if he served Messrs Laeisz with brilliant consistency, they backed him to the hilt, too. Robert Hilgendorf had at least a wonderful flair for learning the lessons of the sea.

The tracks of many of his voyages are known but to plot them is meaningless, for his secret was the single-minded pursuit of the basic know-how of his profession – understanding the sea winds as he needed them, and predicting their changes. He was a consistent and indefatigable observer, with his cold blue eyes that missed nothing and his cold, analytical mind so thoroughly stored with the know-how of wind-change at sea. For there *are* signs. There *is* a consistency in the behaviour patterns of ocean winds. The competent shipmaster must begin by observing all these things, and being one move ahead of wind-shifts when they come.

One advantage helped him which was absent from many masters' careers – he was consistently in the one trade and the one Line, Hamburg outwards to S. Chile with general cargo, homewards from the N. Chile nitrate ports, in good trim both ways, in well-found ships well-manned by competent seamen properly paid and encouraged to stay in their ships by competent owners.

There are some Hilgendorfs among the best yachtsmen of today though there are vast differences between their ship-handling problems and his. The same principles apply in their serious ocean passage making – intense and intelligent application, observation most thorough and never idle, the set of the sails kept at perfection all the time, good morale and reward for effort for a united and experienced crew, not the flutter of a sea-bird nor the movement of a cloud allowed to pass unobserved and not understood. A high standard, indeed: but it can be achieved by the determined, consistently and thoroughly competent, tireless seaman.

No one is born like that, only with the qualities which he may himself develop by his own diligence and strength of character to such a standard. Books of know-how, application to the passing of examinations – these are necessary too. But the real thing is to absorb all the lessons, and know *yourself*, too.

Any master's job is a strain. Especially in an outstanding ship he was very much on show before his knowledgeable world. It is a good idea to be fit for it, physically and mentally.

V

Gone forever?

The big square-rigged ship became in time an anachronism, because men thought her so when, for a brief span in their long history, they had power to burn – rather the sources of power. She had reached a state of development in sailing efficiency, economy and manning and cargo capacity unthought of by previous generations. The second half of the 19th century – perhaps also in a way the first decade of the 20th – saw her at her prime. She was designed, rigged, and built economically and well, and knowledge both of handling her effectively under sail and making useful, economic voyages (with cargoes up to and exceeding 6,000 tons) had increased tremendously. She could make good use of gales short of hurricane force, and the shore 'boffins' had helped her also to defeat long calm, by avoiding it. She could make effective long, non-stop voyages at an average six or seven knots, self-contained and self-sufficient. She served Man and she appealed to men, for she offered a quietly satisfying and at the same time challenging way of life. She sailed with quiet grace and she could be beautiful.

Yet by the third decade of the 20th century, her numbers had shrunk to a few score mainly under the Finnish flag and the German, and most of these obtained cargoes because their capital investment and running costs were then very low. There still survived a sufficient nucleus of competent men (by no means all old) to command and sail them, and a flow of stout youth to handle them, for the tradition was not yet quite broken. Her need was wind and the Lord provided this for the intelligent seeker. She was self-sufficient in port (if allowed to be), and self-contained at sea. She could challenge men greatly but her reward for them could be a great peace – peace of mind and peace of spirit.

Really effective big sailing-ships usefully performing some of the world's work had flourished briefly, in the long history of man's fight with the sea. The economic, large square-rigged ship lasted at most half a century, and the big schooners – the great American ocean-going four- and five-masters – for less. These had followed a host of little wind-blown tramps which wandered far and wide on the short-sea and deep-sea trades, carrying small cargoes rather slowly. They were sufficient for the mood and the economy of their day: very briefly then came the idea of driving swift ships, long and lean and over-sparred – the so-called, greatly publicised 'clippers' which clipped along, hard-driven graceful hulls under a glorious press of sail spread upon too-short spars on too-high masts, fragile with boomed out studding-sails like wings, racing to catch some tea auction or wool sales or to deliver hopeful golddiggers to Australia or California.

These were marvellous, though some were noisy, braggart ships with much of the same kind of masters; their soft-wood hulls were so mercilessly driven that they were unable to sustain a reasonable working life, for they became sodden in the sea, and strained. Soon the driver standing in the midst of those sea-born pyramids of white splendour was aware that he was strained, too: his ship and his own reputation though briefly glorious could not last, nor could the high-pitched, specialised trade to sustain them. Steadily the smoke-belching steamship was cutting into their profitable trades, while men and nations of capital found it worthwhile to finance armies to dig continent-slicing ditches giving the powered ship even greater advantages.

But the big sailing-ship was by then doomed, without the cutting of the Suez Canal. Increased efficiency in boilers and engines had seen to that although then, as always, those most concerned failed to heed what they did not want to notice. Man would always have sense enough to use the free ocean winds, wouldn't he? Well, yes, maybe for a while: indeed, a very long while, in years. But that is all gone now in the 1970's, with a dreadful finality.

To be restored – if ever – it must be firstly in men's minds, the whole idea, possibility, effectiveness and know-how of harnessing the ocean winds. The ocean-world is designed for the use of great sailing-ships, handled by men reared and graduated in their understanding. And now all gone – well, perhaps, not quite all. In 1975 there are fewer than 50 such men left on earth, perhaps three in the United States all in their late 80's or 90's, another ten or a dozen in France and Germany, a dozen more in Finland, one in Chile: none at all in Britain. Don Roberto Miethe in Chile at 97 was oldest and greatest of them all, for he handled the *Potosi* in the Chilean nitrate trade from Hamburg, and that meant four roundings of the Horn each year, two in winter, two to the westwards. His secret? Beginning low and young, sharp-eyed and willing, his mind unhampered by too much 'learning' though properly grounded in the essential things: of good stock, brought up hard, and always willing to develop the abilities of his hands and of his mind. He was finished with school at 12, but never with learning.

The *Potosi* was no gentle clipper with gossamer sails and silken rigging, racing yachtlike through tropic seas. These had their beauty, their stirring triumphs and their value, and swiftly lived out their brief lives only to be thrown into the discard by an Egyptian ditch. The whole of the Laeisz 'P' Line (which included the ultimate in sail, the *Potosi* and *Preussen*) was built up long after the Suez Canal was established, and survived Panama too. The last of them was still sailing long after the Second World War. Two still survive in the mid-'70's, the four-masted barques *Passat* at Travemunde in Germany, and *Pommern* at Mariehamn in Finland, well kept up and in good order but no longer going to sea.

How shall one preserve in writing the skills, flair, and

knowledge acquired by men such as Miethe, Nissen, Piening and the rest? The Williams and the Hughes, the Lewises and the Powells, the Jones and Parrs of Wales? The Learmonts, the MacDonalds, the Gordons of Scotland, de Cloux of Finland, a score Bretons of the great French 'Bounty' ships, the Woodgets and hundreds more of England? It is not possible. All those men began young, lived and sailed hard and long: few wrote anything not in their official or deck logs or letters home. They were graduates of a hard and demanding life they gladly accepted, handed on to them by generations reaching back into antiquity, which was for centuries the *only* way upon the seas for Man at all. They learned the hard way: they fitted in and they accepted hardships, traditions, a great ability, and a way of life now discarded. This could include risks, some fatal.

Well, they accepted all that. They did their part and they departed, having served ships well, and Mankind. Their need was wind, and the Lord provided this for the intelligent seeker. They consumed nothing save the few tons of stores and food they carried with them. They destroyed nothing and they polluted nothing: the wind in their rigging sang songs of fulfilment in men's minds, for the life they gave those who sailed and handled them was real and splendidly fulfilling.

If you think to follow them, consult their Shades. But a heedless, 'entertainment'-crazed civilisation let them go, not even aware of the loss. The pieces cannot be picked up and fitted together again now, nor are auxiliaries any answer. Give a man power and he wants more: high masts of spars are motoring obstructions for they impede power-driven speed. The auxiliary leads inevitably to the full-powered ship: you are back with a natural nothing. There are schemes today for patent ships such as an ingenious but still (after years of work) highly theoretical *dyna-schiff*, a sort of floating gadget driven by six or eight tripod masts of aerofoils radar-controlled for shifts of wind, while computers assess their ideal setting, the masts stepped (if that be the word) on turntables, the aerofoils brailing mechanically into the hollow masts as the wind increases. All startlingly imaginative! But still unbuilt in the mid-1970's and, very probably, likely to remain so. For this ingenious package may ask too much of God, and man.

And yachts? These sail by the scores of thousands now over all the seas of this earth, except perhaps north of Siberia. They give recreation and enjoyment to millions of fortunate people of many nationalities. For what they are, they can often be highly efficient and also beautiful. But the purpose of their high, near-perfect sails is to propel sweet-lined hulls carrying nothing, achieving something indeed in challenge, recreation, pure joy: but doing no work at all and able to do none. You cannot combine their lovely hulls with carrying capacity, for they are for that (or any other working purpose) merely toys. And, after all, how well do the best of them perform, as sailing machines? Of recent years there have been highly publicised ocean voyages organised for yachts, at least one 'race' right round the world (in four passages – U.K. to the Cape, Cape to Sydney, Sydney to Rio, Rio Home, to use the old sailing-ship expressions) in which the word 'clipper' was much used, perhaps little understood. All these yachts had to do was to skim across the sea's face *fast*. One noted that they left the real clipper times unshaken, for the best passage any made counting sailing time only was 124 sailing days for the round voyage. The real clippers did as well and sometimes better than that. Consider the beautiful *Thermopylae's* 60 days from the Channel to Melbourne.

Perhaps more significant, the big, cargo-carrying sailing-ships of the type often contemptuously called windjammers have done at least as well, and more than once. Consider the performances of the heavy, 3,000-ton German four-masted barques *Priwall* (Captain Claus) and *Padua* (Captain Jurs) which both sailed in 1934 from the mouth of the Elbe River in Germany to Spencer Gulf in S. Australia in 65 days. These were not racing ships tuned and manned for that or any other occasion. They were plain working four-masted barques, each manned mainly by comparatively inexperienced youngsters, and only just enough of them; they were simply making the best possible use of the winds the Lord gave them on a normal, well-known, commercial passage. The *Padua* did 351 miles one noon-to-noon day, the *Priwall's* best was 317. In one period of 18 days, both of them averaged a steady 271 miles each day. Homewards, our own big sea-bashing *Parma* – a big steel four-masted barque of honest Scots design and lineage which none would call a clipper, for she was a plain later-day Cape Horn 'windjammer' if ever there were one, built in 1902 – sailed from Port Broughton well inside Spencer Gulf in South Australia to anchorage in Falmouth Bay in 1933 in 83 days. As far as one knows or has ever heard, that was the best working windjammer cargo-carrying run this century. It was not bursts of exceptional speed or great days' runs that did it, for her best noon-to-noon day was just a mile short of 300. She was carrying over 5,000 tons of bagged grain. She had two outstanding qualities both unusual in such a large carrier – she kept steerage-way with the flap of her sails, and she hated to stop. She steered well, handled well, was no wetter in great seas than most heavy four-masted barques, and she rarely killed anyone – no one at all while de Cloux sailed her.

I was there, understudying de Cloux, for I was one of the owners of the *Parma* and planned next to buy a square-rigger of my own, to bring under the British flag. I had been A.B. with that great sailor before in two other four-masted barques, both (under him) outstanding – the former Scots *Lawhill* and the big ex-German school-ship *Herzogin Cecilie*. In 1933 I was abaft the mast, and really learned. Some other ship-masters declared that de Cloux was a 'troll', a sort of wizard with occult powers who could make the wind do his bidding. If he had any particular flair or special aptitude (apart from his indefatigable energy and ceaseless care of ship, crew, and the set of the sails) it was for finding good wind. He claimed no great day's runs, no 'records'. It was his youthful successor who claimed a noon-to-noon 360 for the *Herzogin Cecilie*: de Cloux's best with her was 330. (That same youthful successor lost the *Cecilie* one Channel night not much later.)

Our big *Parma*, that honest, competent Scot with the Italian name, just kept on going at a steady 210 to 260 miles a sea-day (23 hours or so) – four days from the Gulf to off the south of Tasmania, 10 to the 180th meridian, 30 to the Horn after 6,306 sailing miles on our log, which gave us an average of 9 knots – very good going – though the best noon-to-noon run was 263. So we swept on into the S. Atlantic, ever watchful for zones of calm – the worst enemy. We crossed the Line 56 days out, with an excellent four-days passage through those baffling airs and squalls of the Doldrums. Even a poor north-east trade did not stop the faithful old sea-horse, though our best days' run in both Trades was only 190 miles, our worst 65. (It's the *not-stopping* that counts, far more than a few lucky good days' runs.) If we had had fresh Trades we'd have made the Lizard in perhaps a day or two under 80 days, as the 2,000-ton four-masted barque *Swanhilda* is recorded to have done in 1894 (66 days say the books, with what precision one does not know). No matter about that for she must have been very fortunate: 83 days 5 hours was good enough for us.

We romped into Falmouth Bay and let go the hook, and there were the *L'Avenir*, *Pamir* and *Herzogin Cecilie* which had all sailed long before us, the *H.C.* by almost four weeks.

'Aha!' they all said, 'but de Cloux can *troll*,' and shrugged their shoulders as if to say that such occult stuff was beyond them. They were well aware that it was not 'trolling' that had clinched the matter, but the indefatigable determination and tireless skill of a very able man. The *Pamir's* crowd had been swaggering round the pretty port, declaring that they'd 'won' the grain race, for they'd had an excellent passage of 92 days.

De Cloux is dead now, and his ships have gone. He had been the first Finn – the first foreign master – I had sailed with, many years earlier. In that, I count myself most fortunate. I had been with one other splendid master before that and one only – the excellent Murdo' Murchison of the old barque *James Craig*, in the Pacific intercolonial trade. The Scot and the Finn opened my eyes, and I stayed in sail. There were no more sailing Scots so I went back with the Åland Finns when I could, and stayed with them. The *Parma* herself did not last much longer, for de Cloux had to hand her over to a brother-in-law who was perhaps not quite the same kind of man. She began to have expensive accidents, hitting a tug and a dock wall while under tow in Scotland, after a long passage during which a boy was lost. Grain charters, low enough before, fell lower. So the good *Parma* was sold for scrap.

There is far more to square-rigger sailing skill than ever may be put in books, small or large. The real text-books were planned and produced for the thoroughly initiated and the experienced, on their way to becoming certificated officers. They put into few and simple words what the candidates already knew, to help them pass examinations: the least that any such candidate had served at sea before sitting an examination was four years, often all of it in Cape Horn ships. When no longer compulsory, these were still well recognised as the real basis of seafaring, and many great steamship companies in Britain (and all in Germany and Scandinavia) insisted for many years that their deck officers be trained in deepsea square-rig sail. That died in Britain long ago: now (in 1975) all genuine non-powered such ships have long been gone. How then may their skills be handed on? Some square-rigged school-ships (though also full-powered motor-ships) may help cadets a little and officers a good deal: but power in a sailing-ship is an insidious thing, often fatal and at times treacherous to real sailing. Planned 'schedules' follow, fitted into the imagined (or real) needs of shore academies or committees. The beautiful square-rigged ship on schedule, full of valuable lads, is no longer even the agent of the great ocean winds but of that unworkable and unimaginative abomination, the dictatorial committee. Many still do a splendid best, notably the barquentine *Captain Scott* in northern British waters, the Danes, *Danmark* and *Georg Stage*, Norwegians, and Germans, the U.S. Coastguard with the barque *Eagle* especially when she has a really interested captain in command of her, which by God's grace and the excellence of the Coast Guard's traditions, is often.

But as for the non-powered big square-rigged ship getting on quietly (noisily enough in gales) with something of the world's real work, she is now gone from a heedless world for ever – not so much discarded with all her challenging skills and splendid performance, as allowed quietly to disappear and the loss not even noticed.

She has gone for ever, one must fear, for men may not throw long-fostered skills away in the sea, and find them again. You cannot break great traditions and mend them later at will. And, worst of all, you cannot restore the tranquility of an age which accepted (not only at sea) Nature's wind as power.

Glossary

belaying pin. Wood or iron pin (smooth, short rod) round which sailing ships' gear was secured by turns.

bowsprit. The spar (sprit) at the bow of a sailing ship.

buntlines. Lines (rope or wire) across the belly of a square sail which are hauled up to subdue the canvas when taking in.

flunkeying. Acting as a 'flunkey', or servant.

forecastle head. Built up fore-part of the deck, immediately abaft the cutwaters.

hawse. Part of hull for'ard where the anchor cables emerge from the bow through the hawse-pipes: the angle between the ship and the lead of cable when at anchor.

Horse latitudes. Zones of shifting winds and calms at S. and N. limits of Trade Winds.

jigger. Fourth mast in a large sailing ship.

lateen sail. Fore-and-aft triangular sail set on a boom hoisted on a mast, as in a dhow.

leechline. Rope for hauling up the leeches (sides) of a square sail.

loblollying. In former days, unskilled assistants to ships' surgeons were loblolly boys.

mizzenmast. Third mast in a sailing ship.

pin rail. Wooden rail built at convenient height, bored to accept belaying pins.

reef points. Short pieces of rope sewn to a sail for securing a tuck (reef) in it.

royal. Uppermost square sail in square-riggers without skysails.

spritsail. A sail set on (or stretched by) a sprit, either a small square-sail set on a yard across the bowsprit or a fore-and-aft sail on a sprit set up abaft the mast, diagonally, as in a Thames barge.

topgallant. Square sail immediately below the royal, which is uppermost (unless a skysail is carried).

trysail. Stout triangular sail usually set well aft, used generally to hold the ship's head up to a gale when hove to.

vang. Simple tackles for holding the gaff steady, helping with the setting of the spanker.

williwaws. Puffs of rapidly shifting winds.

windlass. Device for performing heavy work such as raising an anchor in a ship, usually worked by hand-power in sailing ships.

Recommended books for the interested

THE sailing-ship era produced many books, professional text books often very technical, books of reminiscences and of yarns, moving accounts of voyages, of wrecks, of 'clippers' and their races, Cape Horners and their trials. These began in the Bible and are not ended yet. The crammers' books which candidates used to pass examinations are of little use now the era they served is ended, for they were written for those already knowledgeable in the subject. In any practical sense, the numbers of such seamen surviving now is to be reckoned in a few hundreds, maybe scores. But, until recent years, British candidates presenting themselves for examination in their fitness for Board of Trade certificates of competency as second mate, mate, or master in sail, were required only to produce evidence of having served a twelve-month on the articles of some square-rigged ship.

'On the articles' was the vital matter, for among the last sea-going square-riggers was the little fleet of 'onker' barques in the so-called firewood trade from the Baltic to London. Enterprising young gentlemen, intent on good careers in ships, used to sign on in some of these for the last run of the season, duly signing the all-important 'articles' and sailing aboard the chosen barque to her home-port in the Baltic. Here they left, but their names remained behind them, legally on the Articles. It was (for a while) possible to record the essential year's service in this way with the minimum inconvenience of going to sea. Nor were Scandinavian vessels the only ones involved. The handsome old barquentine *Waterwitch*, though no 'onkerman', provided their sea time to others, and it was said that her Articles were often better manned than her decks.

These good youngsters, being bright, learned fast. It was inefficient shore authority which insisted on such outmoded qualifications. It was all fair enough: they were never going to use their 'Sail endorsement' except for the few who might be called upon as pilots to bring a square-rigger into the London River. There, her own master would do the handling under sail. It was not necessary for the pilot to do that at all, except to be able to judge what the square-rigger could do and could not do. This was a considerable help: they served very well.

They found the books useful, too. So would anyone today who had seen service in excellent school-ships like the Danish ships *Danmark* and *Georg Stage* which, though low-powered auxiliaries sailing to schedules, are still handled properly, and the Norwegian ship *Sörlandet* too, and a few others including Germany's barque *Gorch Fock* and Poland's *Dar Pomorza*. All these, and the U.S. Coast Guard's training barque *Eagle*, do as good a sailing job as they may, but one difficulty for many of them is that inevitably the schedule at times has to mean more than the sailing, and the committees of management know very well about their big diesels. (So do wives.)

You can't use the wind on schedule. But you can use the books to increase your knowledge. The old books are long out of print, having no longer relevance, and may be obtained only through specialist dealers in old maritime books, but there is a good market in these. Most of these question-and-answer books were always rather dull reading but the facts are there.

Here is a list of possibly the best, as one remembers them:

Nicholls's Seamanship and Viva Voce Guide by A. E. Nicholls, FRAS, Extra Master. Glasgow, Brown, Son and Ferguson. My edition (1924) contains chapters on 'Sailing a Ship', and 'Management of a Sailing Vessel Under Canvas' which are useful.

Alston's *Seamanship*, Revised and Enlarged by Commander

R. H. Harris RN, 200 Illustrations. London, Simpkin Marshall and Co.: Portsmouth, Griffin and Co., 2 The Hard. 1872. Naval, but square-riggers in the main were handled in standard ways. Interesting and useful; with a 'Treatise on Nautical Surveying' and 'Instructions for Officers of the Merchant Service'.

Modern Seamanship, Austin M. Knight. London, Kegan Paul, Trench Trubner and Co., 1905 (3rd edition). Has excellent chapters on Manoeuvring Under Sail.

Practical Seamanship for Men in the Merchant Service, by John Todd, Master Mariner, Formerly of the Turkish Navy, and W. B. Whall FRAS, Extra Master, Younger Brother of Trinity House, etc. Fifth edition 1904. George Philip and Son Ltd., London. 380-odd pages mainly of interesting information though including some on twin-screw steamers.

The Seaman's Manual, A Treatise on Practical Seamanship: Dictionary of Sea Terms, etc. etc. By R. H. Dana, Jun. My edition, the thirteenth, published by E. Moxon, Son and Co. London, 1873. Many editions: called The Seaman's Friend in USA. Comprehensive, clearly written, and interesting.

There are other good works in my library which I did not have when at sea, such as a slim volume entitled *The Young Shipmaster* by one Joseph Leeman, Master Mariner, etc., Aberdeen, John Avery and Co. Ltd., 1886 (very general: meant for Masters), and an even slimmer effort called simply *Under Square Sail*, by T. M. Withers, 3rd edition, London Pewtress and Co., High Holborn, 1898 (third edition). This brief effort (40 small pages of text, 22 plates) contains an interesting glossary, and describes square-rigger manoeuvres long forgotten, such as 'box-hauling' (which meant wearing a small square-rigger while losing minimum leeway) and 'club-hauling' (tacking in narrow waters, using an anchor to help.)

I never saw nor heard of a ship performing either of these operations which must have been rather desperate.

Modern works

Very useful, general books on big square-riggers, in English, are led by Mr. Harold A. Underhill's excellent *Masting and Rigging: The Clipper Ship and Ocean Carrier*, and *Deep-Water Sail*, both published in Glasgow by Brown, Son and Ferguson, 52 Darnley Street, and still in print. Greatly assisted by Mr. Underhill's precise plans and drawings – he was a skilled draftsman, producing among other things many sets of model-makers' plans for outstanding ships – hese books are excellent, copiously illustrated, and en-cyclopaedic, as also is his *Sailing-Ship Rigs and Rigging* with many useful and interesting plans and drawings.

As for something like clearly comprehensible descriptions of sailing-ship handling, manoeuvring and voyage-making, etc., right to the end of the era, a useful work, I hope, is my own *The Way of a Ship* (Hodder and Stoughton, London) Charles Scribner's Sons, New York, also in Dutch and German. This is illustrated by photographs, diagrams, maps and drawings dealing with both sail-handling and the management of large ships under sail, as well as voyage-making, beating past the Horn and so forth. It is in print, currently in paper-back.

There is also the splendid study of the last of the square-igged ships by Mr W. L. A. Derby, *The Tall Ships Pass* Jonathan Cape, London) who served in the Finnish – ormerly German – four-masted barque *Herzogin Cecilie*. This is a massive work, thorough and reliable. Mr Derby had shipping background as a senior member of Lloyds, and made a voyage in the *Cecilie*. He had an inquiring and in-ormed mind and wide-open eyes.